Return to the Launch Site: My Life Story

By Percy E. Baynes

To all the young men who were in the Great Migration from Caswell County, North Carolina in the early 1950s to Washington, DC, I dedicate *Return to the Launch Site* (RTLS) to you. Your quest for a more rewarding lifestyle than working as sharecroppers and a strong desire to return home with resources to improve the quality of life for your family and friends. RTLS represents your journey as well as mine.

Foreword

Percy began talking about writing a book on his life in 1972. That was the year we moved to Palos Verdes, California with all four of our children. Later that year, the movie *Sounder* was released. While sitting in the theater, I turned to Percy and said, "Somebody already wrote your story." All the stories about hunting rabbits and squirrels in the dark that he told me through the years were suddenly on the large screen in Technicolor. Little did I know that 47 years later, I would have the opportunity to read my husband's book and get to know him in an entirely different way.

Hearing him talk about his family and upbringing did not affect me the way that it did when I began reviewing his manuscript. There was something about seeing his life in writing that made me feel the pain, the joy, the struggles, and the successes with new eyes and appreciation. Maybe there's something about taking a moment when you have a balcony-level view that you are unable to see when living alongside someone for more than 60 years.

My husband is a quiet and reserved man. He is a man of integrity and great faith. I have learned so much more about how he sees the world – which is completely different from me in some ways. We think so differently, and yet it was as though God knew that we were meant to be together.

I believe that when you read this story, you will see that with God all things are possible. Following the plans that God has for you will help you reach your greatest potential and realize your life's purpose. As you read this book, look for the parallels in your own journey and be open for a transformative experience. Enjoy and be blessed!

Dorothy Totten Baynes
July 2019

Introduction

The Space Shuttle was the world's first reusable spacecraft. I was privileged to serve on the team that designed the Orbiter vehicle section, which transported the crew into space and brought them back to Earth. Connected to enormous boosters and an external fuel tank, the craft launched like a rocket and returned to Earth like a glider. For more than 30 years, the shuttles carried crews, satellites, and materials into space and returned items in need of repair. This enabled the construction of the International Space Station and exponentially expanded our understanding of the universe.

As I think about the trajectory of my life, it very much mirrors this operational flight pattern. The power of God to launch me out of the tobacco fields of North Carolina, carry me safely through orbit, and then gently guide me back to the sight of the launch, continues to overwhelm me with joy and gratitude.

Many people do not know my life story. I tried my best to write it—the pages that follow include facts and stories based on my 86 years of memories. Those of you who are part of my story may have different recollections. Just know that I am grateful to each of you, grateful for the journey, and grateful to God, from whom all blessings flow!

Chapter One
1933—The Great Depression

We are hard pressed on every side, but not crushed; perplexed, but not in despair; persecuted, but not abandoned; struck down, but not destroyed.
—2 Corinthians 4:8-9

While no group escaped the economic devastation of the Great Depression, few suffered more than African Americans, who experienced the highest unemployment rate during the 1930s.
—Christopher Klein

It is generally accepted that 1933 was a pivotal year during the Great Depression. Many economists believe that although 1933 was the year that the United States began its recovery, conditions were dire with unemployment peaking at 25.2% in the United States. This disproportionately affected African Americans, who experienced nearly 50% unemployment during that same year. People left their homes looking for work. In Europe, Adolf Hitler became chancellor of Germany and opened the first concentration camp at Dachau. The entire world was in turmoil.

My home state of North Carolina was not immune to the deepening poverty and racial and ethnic violence permeating the country and the world. North Carolina was primarily a rural state, and the majority of African Americans made their living by farming. In Caswell County, African Americans were mostly sharecroppers or worked as hired servants for white landowners. This was a direct vestige of slavery that had legally ended in the United States in 1865. Sharecropping was a system in which freed black citizens continued to farm for white landowners. They could only sell their crops back to the landowners' designated markets that paid them very little. In addition, the landowners created a system of debt (for tools, supplies, and other made-up costs) and sharecroppers could not move or stop farming until their debts were completely satisfied.

My grandfather, George Baynes, was born during slavery in 1861. He too became a sharecropper. However, in 1914, he was somehow able to save enough money to purchase a small 79-acre parcel of land from a white landowner. This was unheard of at the time. Stories of the unusual transaction indicate that because the farm was landlocked and the soil was not very good for producing crops, white farmers probably thought that my grandfather had been tricked out of his hard-saved money. The reality was that the seller, Sidney Florence, was a person that was not in sync with the racist attitudes of the other white landowners. The farm became an oasis for the entire Baynes family. It also provided support for other black families who were forced to move from white landowners' farms because their services were no longer needed.

As Hitler was opening the first concentration camp to execute Jews in Germany, racial violence in the southern United States also began to surge. Even in Northern cities, whites demanded that black employees be fired if there were white people out of work. Lynching, which had decreased to eight in North Carolina in 1932, rose to 28 in 1933.

It was in this same year that Charlie and Mary Baynes, living on the Baynes family farm with his parents, George and Rebecca, welcomed their third child, Percy Elmore Baynes. That son was me, and I am writing this book to record my secular and spiritual journey from 1933 to the present.

The beginning of my journey - My birth home built by my father and grandfather

Chapter Two
The First Three Years—Life and Death

A man's ways seem innocent to him, but motives are weighted by the Lord.
—Proverb 16:2

It takes a whole village to raise a child.
—Nigerian Proverb

Prior to my birth, Charlie and Mary Baynes birthed two children, Sarah Catherine and John William. I was born on a Monday, on May 1, 1933.

Thus, my journey began in our one-room little log cabin with a loft and a lean-to kitchen. My grandfather and father had built the cabin using pine trees from the farm. It was modest to say the least, and the outhouse was approximately 50 yards from the back of the house. The prevailing conditions on the farm were a mirror image of the destitute conditions in the country including limited marketing for farm products as well as very little money in circulation.

Survival was totally a function of what could be produced on the farm. Reflecting with my twenty-first century mind-set, one must wonder why my parents continued to increase their family during such dire times. However, I am grateful that they had faith and hope that there would be better days ahead.

The first three years of my life were characterized by highs and lows. The highs were the joy I experienced with my older siblings. The lows were my mother's illness and eventual death and how it completely changed our lives. Many people often say, "You can't possibly remember your mother," because I was only three years old when she died. However, my memories of mom are deeply etched in my mind and soul.

I can recall actual conversations I had with her. In 1936, she was pregnant with my youngest sister, and she was also very sick. My

12

mom had become blind and everyone in the community was very worried about her. I now know that she had an untreated tumor on her pituitary gland that caused her blindness (a condition that our oldest daughter would inherit but was diagnosed and treated in a timely manner). I remember going outside to play with my brother and sister or visiting with my grandparents and then going back to our house to spend time with mom. During those visits, she would often tell me that she was going to die. At the time, I did not understand that when she died, she would not come back. So, each time I went to see her I would ask, "Are you dead yet?" She would just smile at me and answer, "Not yet."

Sometime early that summer, they took my mother to Duke Hospital in Durham, North Carolina. There were not many hospitals in the state and there was no health insurance that would cover black people. To this day, I do not know how her medical bills were paid. How the adults in my family were able to visit my mother in the hospital nearly 70 miles away was a mystery to me. Later in life, I learned that the minister of Sweet Gum Grove Baptist Church, our local church, owned a reliable car, and he provided transportation for them all the way to Durham and back. In the 1930s, children were not permitted to visit hospitals; only adults. So, we would wait for them to return to hear how she was doing. It was in that hospital that my mother died on August 18, 1936.

One month before her death, on July 18th, she gave birth to my youngest sister Claudia Vernell. Throughout my mother's illness, my grandmother cared for my siblings and me. When my sister came home from the hospital, she went to live in my grandparent's house. I often wonder how my father managed to multitask the way he did, responsible for four small children and working on the farm to produce food for the family. *But for God!_*

When my mother died, it was the practice of the time to take the body to the house after embalming. I remember my mom's body lying in the coffin in our little log home, occupying the space where her bed had once been located. My father lifted me up so that I could see her body up close. It is painful to recall this experience, but I don't remember being sad at the time. Her body remained in the house overnight and the next day she was taken to the church for the funeral. Following the funeral, my mom, Mary Baynes, was buried in the church cemetery, under a sweetgum tree.

My Mom - Mary Florence Baynes

Chapter Three
Life without Mom

The Lord is near to those who are broken-hearted and saves those who are crushed in spirit.
—Psalm 34:18

I really saw clearly, and for the first time, why a mother is really important. Not just because she feeds and also loves and cuddles and even mollycoddles a child, but because in an interesting and maybe an eerie and unworldly way she stands in the gap. She stands between the unknown and the known.
—Maya Angelou

After the death of my mother, we moved into the "big house" with my grandparents. My father, siblings, and I joined two other relatives that were already living with them; Katie Mae Pattillo and my first cousin, Giles Richmond, Jr. (also known as June). My grandmother became a mother to all the kids. Although my memory during this time is not as clear, I am told that my behavior was awful. I was probably angry that my mother had died, and at three years old did not know how to express it. Eventually, my behavior was so bad, that my brother John and I were sent to live with my uncle and aunt, Coy and Lucy Malone. That arrangement worked well for my brother John, but it only lasted for two weeks for me. My father came to pick me up, and John stayed with them for another month or so. We were all grieving in our own ways and trying to figure out what life would be like without mom.

Upon returning to my grandparent's home, I was assigned various chores such as feeding the pigs and cows and helping to maintain the yard work near the house. Looking back, they were probably trying to keep me busy in order to keep me out of trouble. It was also during this time that I became very close to my father's favorite sister, Aunt Myrtle.

Aunt Myrtle worked in Burlington, North Carolina as a live-in domestic for a white family during the week. She would return to

15

the farm on weekends. We were always very happy to see her when she came home because she would bring us used clothes her employers gave her. One time, she brought a tricycle for our youngest sister Vernell. We were all so excited as we took turns pushing her across the farmyard. Back then, our toys consisted of things we could make from spare parts produced or found on the farm. We made go-carts from small trees and used larger trees to make the wooden wheels. During this time, gasoline-powered vehicles were replacing the horse and buggy as the mode of travel. So, we also played on the old buggies riding down the hills on the farm. I never owned a bicycle, a go-kart (other than the one we made), or any of the other ride-on toys that many people may think of when they recall their childhoods. Those types of toys inspired little boys to dream of becoming race car drivers or pilots. When I reflect on those early experiences, I am clear that a greater *power* was directing my path to pursue not just Earth-based transportation systems but space-based ones as well.

When I was six, my dad enrolled me in the first grade at Anderson Elementary School. In the late 1930s, schools were segregated and not equal. Don't get me wrong, we still had some of the most amazing teachers. But they taught with very few books and supplies that are typically needed to educate children. This was an eye-opening experience as I joined other six year olds in a setting that consisted of seven classes in one room. The state and county provided transportation to elementary schools for white children but not black children. So, we walked three miles each way to and from school every day. (Later in life, when I told these stories to my own children, they'd eventually laugh and say, "We know, we know. It was three miles, uphill, in the snow, barefoot, both ways!") I owe a belated thanks to Mrs. Odessa Brown, my teacher for seven years in that one-room school. I still marvel at how she was able to accomplish the many tasks she performed, while teaching children at so many different grade levels.

In 1941, the Japanese attacked Pearl Harbor and the United States initiated an all-out mobilization to support the ongoing war in Europe. The mobilization directly impacted what we produced on my grandfather's farm. Farm equipment, including chicken coop wire, were rationed and only sold to "eligible" farmers (which did not include black farmers who farmed their own land.) A rationing system was also instituted that restricted what people could buy in the marketplace. For example, sugar was the first consumer product rationed. Each household could only buy up to .5 pounds of sugar per week. Even the production of clothes stopped, so that cotton and other materials could be dedicated to uniforms and other war-related items. During that time, we had to make most of our clothes out of burlap feed bags and anything else we could find. The State of North Carolina was still deep in the economic depression. And yet my youthful attitude was one of excitement. The young men of draft age were called to service and I recall how thrilling it was seeing them return home in uniform and hearing their stories of faraway places and people. Clearly, I knew nothing about the dangers of war.

During the war era (1941–1946), we survived by carefully managing the produce from the farm and any clothing we were able to purchase. My grandfather provided the opportunity for another family to live in my birth house (log home) and to work as sharecroppers. The rationing of cloth and material directly impacted the style of clothes that were available to civilians. There was a suit style called the "Zoot" suit, which was popular among African Americans after they were made popular by jazz performers such as Cab Calloway. The pants were high-waisted, wide-legged and tight cuffed. The blazers had wide padded shoulders, a wide lapel and were long enough to hit a man in the middle of his thighs. I could only dream of owning such a suit!

In 1943, the death angel visited the Baynes family again. My grandfather, George W. Baynes died at the age of eighty-two. He lived a life that I wanted to emulate. He was a disciple of Jesus Christ and shared the Bible with me at an early age. At my age of ten, I confessed Christ as my Savior and was baptized at Sweet Gum Baptist Church. However, that is not where the story ends. My faith journey was just beginning.

In 1946, the death angel came yet again. This time it was my grandmother, Rebecca H. Baynes, who died at the age of eighty. As I reflect, this was a sad time for my thirteen-year-old self. My grandmother had become my mother, and now she was gone too. As grief-stricken as I was, I think I felt worse for my father. In the span of a few short years, he had become solely responsible for three teens and a preteen. Yet, he stepped up to the plate and provided leadership to our family in marvelous and extraordinary ways.

My Grandparent's home – "The Big House"

Chapter Four
My Dad Led the Way

God has made him your father for a reason, and you will be blessed for honoring him.
—Exodus 20:12

My father didn't tell me how to live; he lived and let me watch him do it.
—Clarence B. Kelland

My father was a strong and quiet man, who was one of the hardest workers I have ever known. He was also a man of great faith and deeply loved his family. When our mother died, followed by granddad, and then grandma, he became our anchor and our sail.

We were fortunate to have extended family living nearby. Uncle Giles Thomas ("Tom") Baynes lived just across the hill from us. Uncle Tom was a World War I veteran who served in France. Upon returning from his service he began sharecropping on the Fitch farm. Mr. Fitch was the county deputy sheriff in Caswell County. It was reported that the Sheriff was able to get the farm that Uncle Tom lived on for only $750 (60 acres) through tax liens (an early case of insider trading). When I was young, I thought Uncle Tom owned his farm. I should have known better because for many years he only owned one mule and a carol (which is what we called a wagon designed for one mule). He later purchased another mule and a wagon designed for two mules.

In contrast, my father owned a Ford Model T during his early life. The Model T was built by Ford from 1908 to 1927 on the revolutionary assembly lines created by Henry Ford. As a result, the car was more affordable to the common man for a price as low as $300. However, the common man did not often include black people, and $300 was more than half of what sharecroppers were paid for their annual tobacco crops. Somehow, my father figured out how to navigate well financially.

In 1938, when I was five years old, Uncle Tom's wife died during childbirth, leaving him to raise my cousins Irvin (then 16), Nelly, Milther, Charlie D. (also known as CD), Waddell, and Maude. Our two families became one and we formed a close relationship which has continued throughout our lives. I still consider Nellie and Maude, the only two of Uncle Tom's children still living, my sisters. The highlight of all of us living together in Uncle Tom's house was the role that Maude and Vernell played. They were responsible for preparing supper (the last meal of the day). *What a treat*!

It was during that same year that my dad again broke from the norm for most blacks living in the South and bought his next car—a 1934 Chevrolet. We knew that it was the number one choice of cars for the year! The funny thing is that my dad did not even know how to drive it. Whenever he wanted to go somewhere, he had someone else to drive for him. On one fourth Sunday in May, we all loaded into the car and Isaac Richmond drove us to church. I will never forget that day because all eyes were on Charlie Baynes, his kids, and that big black Chevy. We drove up to Sweet Gum Baptist Church as though we were wealthier than we really were. During that time, most people walked everywhere, or they still used horses and buggies. The church yard was lined with buggies that Sunday and I was so proud to be Charlie Baynes's son! My dad never really learned to drive that car; he eventually was in an accident in Burlington, and there was so much damage that he ended up parking the car in the barnyard, where it stayed.

Some years later, a man that was leaving to serve in the military had a 1932 Chevy for sale, and my dad bought it from him. During World War II, cars were scarce. The car assembly plants were converted into factories to produce weapons and other items needed for the soldiers. An interesting fact—between 1942 and 1945, no cars were built in the United States at all, so civilians could not buy new cars. Thus, despite the 1932 Chevy being older than the 1934 Chevy rusting in the barnyard, my dad was thrilled to buy it and so were we. He drove the 1932 Chevy for a while and as things broke down, it became more and more difficult to find parts to make repairs. After that, the car was also moved into the barnyard, and then my dad found another man who was selling a 1931 Chevy, and he bought it. We seemed to be going backward, but this one lasted a long time. When I was fifteen and a half years old, I learned to drive in the 1932 Chevy and got my driver's license.

In the 1930s and 1940s, a family's success was measured by their ability to own a car. Even though we owned the 1931 Chevy, when I was in high school, I told people that my dad also owned a 1940 Chevy to impress them. There was one guy in my class who had attended elementary school with me and he always corrected me saying that it was just a 1931 Chevy. He was my truth-finder and he is still alive today. Thanks, Bob Jones, for always setting the record straight.

While working with dad on the farm, he tried to motivate us, saying, "Work hard, because I think I see a 1940 Chevy sitting at the end of that row of tobacco." My brother John and I would pick up our pace and work as hard as we could. There was just something about owning a nice car. My Uncle Tom was not able to afford to buy a car until 1952, when he purchased a 1950 Ford. (Interestingly, later in life, when I could afford expensive luxury cars, I still gravitated to much more practical family vehicles like our station wagon.)

My brother John and I always held an affinity for each other. He was very strong, and he taught me a lot of things. We developed a technique where we'd hold one foot out in front of us and holding it with the opposite hand we'd then jump through the formed circle with the leg that we were balancing on. We were the only boys in our entire community who could accomplish this feat! In addition to the fun we created, John was also an unusually hard worker. My dad really looked to him as the one who would run the farm one day. In fact, if dad had lived longer, John probably would have become a lifelong farmer. On the contrary, my desire was to move on. We lived on an isolated, landlocked farm, a quarter of a mile from the state highway. We usually did not see other people except our cousins across the hill; so, seeing other children our age was exciting. We looked forward to the biannual "Homecomings" at Sweet Gum Baptist Church that took place fourth Sunday in May and October. For some reason, our baby sister Vernell seemed to always get sick on those fourth Sundays and we'd have to stay home with her. John and I would be madder than mad!

However, even if we missed the big meetings at Sweet Gum, in our community, the "Association" (which we called the "Socation" pronounced so-sa-tion) was the biggest event of the year! All the local churches would come together and worship for three days. It took place every year during the first week in August, before the farmers harvested their tobacco. For years, it had rotated between various host churches until the Association purchased property in Yanceyville, North Carolina as a permanent place for the gathering, which also boasted an expanded campground. Before the harvest, none of us had a lot of money, so we spent the entire summer helping other farmers, earning as much as $3–$5 per day. Our goal was to work all summer and save our money to spend at the Association. Many people stayed on the grounds in little houses erected behind the main building and some even slept in tents. For us, the best day was on Friday when we got to see all our friends from school. Back then, it was unheard of to go to places like Raleigh, Greensboro, or even Burlington on a regular basis. People just did not travel and move around that much.

After the Association each year, we harvested our tobacco. The Tobacco Market was in Danville, Virginia. My father didn't have a vehicle large enough to transport the tobacco. Some years he used the horse and wagon to go all the way to Danville. He'd have to spend two or three nights and there were no hotels for black people in Danville. My father either slept in our wagon or on a pallet in the corner of the tobacco warehouse. I never got to go with him. Thinking back, he probably didn't want his children to be subjected to the arbitrary and dangerous violence girded by Jim Crow laws and racist attitudes. In later years, he hired someone with a trailer to pull the tobacco behind the car, but we still never went to Danville with him.

My Dad Charlie Baynes in 1946

Clockwise from the top: My siblings - John, Vernell, and Me on the patio at our home in Maryland; Our sister Catherine; Vernell and our cousin June; Cousins Maude, Nellie, Waddell, and me at their church in New Jersey.

Chapter Five
The Epiphany—June 6, 1949

There the angel of the Lord appeared to him in flames of fire from within a bush.
—Exodus 3:2

If you look throughout human history the central epiphany of every religious tradition always occurs in the wilderness.
—John F. Kennedy

I turned sixteen on May 1, 1949. Just over a month later, on June 6, 1949, Charlie Baynes departed the earth. My father died on a Sunday morning. He was ill throughout the night and died early the next day. During the night before he died, my sisters Catherine, Vernell, and I were in the house with him. He was sick for months; he had lost a lot of weight and was very weak. He was probably down to about 120 pounds at this point. At 4 am that Sunday morning, we realized he was dying. Catherine ran to Uncle Tom's house to get help. By the time they returned, dad had already died. Right before my very eyes, the man who held what was left of our family together, took his last breath.

Shortly before his health began rapidly declining, we learned that dad had cancer. He was a smoker most of his life and cancer had poisoned his lungs. Cancer was not a well-known disease at the time, and the health dangers of smoking were not known to the public for another fifteen years when a report was released by the U.S. Surgeon General in 1964. It took another six years, in 1970, for companies to begin posting health warnings on tobacco products. The tobacco we planted and harvested annually that financially supported our family was also the same product that killed our dad.

When dad began losing weight, we scheduled an appointment for him to go to Duke Hospital to see a doctor. This was the same hospital where my mother died. His cousin, David Bigelow, drove us to the hospital. I was sixteen years old when he received his cancer diagnosis. Unlike during my mom's illness, I was now old

25

enough to go into the hospital with him. The doctors said that he needed to be hospitalized, but they did not have a "colored patient" bed for him. They promised to call us when a bed became available. We gave them the phone number for the Baynes General Store, as that was the only place where we could receive a phone message. The Baynes General Store, like many of the businesses, churches and roads in our community were named after the white Baynes family. Although we have never been able to trace our complete family history, many of us believe that the name Baynes derived from the Baynes plantation during slavery. The white Baynes family once owned the black Baynes family.

Later that morning after my father died, I was so distraught that I walked down behind the house and just laid in the gully. I began screaming an angry prayer to God, saying, "God, you have taken my dad and you have taken my mom! You have made me an orphan! Why not take me?! Why leave me here?!" Tears were streaming down my face, my heart ached with resentment, and I was blinded by the intensity of the sun and the moment. Just then, a spirit came upon me and said, "Your father has lived his life, and that he has done. You have yours yet to live." To be honest, it was the most frightening experience of my life! The voice was clear coming from nowhere yet coming from everywhere. I got out of that gully as quickly as I could and sprinted back to the house. The experience and words stuck with me in the days leading up to the funeral. "Your father has lived his life, and that he has done. You have yours yet to live."

It was a very sad time for us because it happened on June 6th, and normally by that time farmers were getting ready to start cultivating the tobacco crops. Our family had not planted any tobacco or any other grains in the year 1949. We were waiting to take the lead from dad, because he always told us what to do. The night my father died, we had $15 total for our entire household. It was all the money we had, and we only had that because we were raising and selling piglets. A farmer had come the day before my father died and paid us $15.

Dad was buried that Wednesday, following his death on Sunday. On the day of his funeral, Duke Hospital called the Baynes General Store and said they had a "colored patient" bed ready for him. John was eighteen, Catherine was twenty, and Vernell was only twelve.

After the funeral, John and I decided to stay in the house that night. We went upstairs where we always slept. But on this night, lots of rats, as big as squirrels, came into the house. It seemed like every rat on earth came into the house and we could hear them all night long. The next morning, we decided to move to Uncle Tom's house. Uncle Tom became a father for John, June, Vernell, and me. He was a caring and kind man, and he provided for us in the same way he provided for his own children.

The day after the funeral, on a Thursday morning, farmers from all over our community came in wagons, cars, and on foot to our farm, and they planted all our tobacco in that one day. That's how we got our crop planted that year. The entire community came together; some as far as five and ten miles away, but they did come. I remember thinking all during this time about my prayer, "You have taken my father and my mother. Why leave me here? Why not take me?" All of this happened during that one week in 1949. We continued cultivating the crop by plowing and weeding until it was time to harvest.

Shortly after the community salvaged our livelihood, I received a card from the principal of Caswell County Training School saying that I had been selected as a school bus driver. Back then, the county and state provided buses to transport black students to and from the segregated high school. He instructed me to pick up the bus on a specific day in August. This was a major change in my life. First, we now had transportation. I caught a ride into Yanceyville to pick up the bus. I served as the school bus driver in 1949 and 1950. Second, this was a huge step forward for me. Prior to becoming the bus driver, we walked about 2.5 miles to get to the bus. Now, I could park the bus at Uncle Tom's house, where we all lived. Maybe things were starting to turn around.

Living with Uncle Tom and my cousins was an experience I greatly enjoyed. Yet, at the end of that school year, there was still this burning desire within me, and I continued to remember the epiphany I experienced in the gully, "He has lived his life, that he has done. You have yours yet to live."

At this point, I had resigned myself to stay on the farm. I was going to step up and become a big farmer, just like my dad. In the spring of 1950, I went through the process of planting the next crop. Before his death, dad had entered into an agreement to buy the farm from his siblings. In order to pay it off, he still owed $850. Uncle Tom made a deal with a white businessman, Mr. Oliver, who had a sawmill and harvested logs. Mr. Oliver agreed to pay $800 to cut down the trees on the farm. He also ran a country store over on Highway 62. Uncle Tom told me to stop by the store and tell Mr. Oliver that we needed $50 more to close the deal. At the age of sixteen, on my way home, after dropping the students off, I stopped by Mr. Oliver's store and negotiated my first business deal. Mr. Oliver agreed to pay the additional $50 for a total of $850. He then moved his sawmill to our farm to harvest the logs. John and CD both got jobs working at the sawmill.

I turned 17 years old that May. This was significant, because back then when the boys turned 17, we each received our own one-acre allotment of tobacco. It was almost like a rite of passage into manhood. They were preparing us to be financially independent so that we could take care of future wives and children. (When writing this book, I realized that this was not provided for the girls in the family. Although this would be completely unacceptable now, the thinking then was that the girls would marry, and their husbands would provide for them.)

One day I was driving over to the farm after delivering all the schoolchildren safely home. It was just getting dark and as I drove up, I saw a silhouette of John and CD walking to the house from the sawmill. I was so moved at that moment that I thought that I really could take over the farm and be a farmer. Maybe this is what the Lord had in store for me. "You have yours left to live."

To further support this notion, Allen Baynes, one of my dad's cousins who lived in Mebane, came to visit one day at Uncle Tom's house. At some point during that school year, I changed my mind and decided that I wanted to leave the farm and get an education to become a doctor. In my mind I felt that I needed to study medicine, because I had personally witnessed my mother and father suffer so much without appropriate medical care. During his visit, Allen said to me, "This farm life is the best life you will ever have. You should stay."

This tormented me for many days, but in the end, I was still determined to move on. My brother John decided to leave the farm in December 1949 to move to DC in the hopes of finding a better paying job. His decision to leave made me once again rethink leaving the farm. Someone needed to run it.

However, in the spring of 1950, something dramatic occurred. On the farm, there were no radios or ways to communicate with the outside world. I subscribed to the *Greensboro Daily News* and picked it up from the mailbox every day. In June 1950, the newspaper headlines declared that North Korea passed the 38 parallel and that a war was commencing between North and South Korea. The United States announced that it would be supporting South Korea. Even though war was looming, I was happy, because I knew that war and the military were another avenue for me to leave the farm. I recalled the soldiers from World War II, who had returned to our community and shared so much of what they saw and experienced around the world. I was seventeen and I was now going to be eligible to serve my country. I was just as happy as could be—a way out! Sure enough the draft was reenacted again.

In the fall of 1950, I sold the tobacco that had been planted in the spring. Normally, when selling tobacco, the strategy was to space out your sales over several weeks in order to control the supply and maximize the sales amount. My first solo tobacco sale took place in Durham, North Carolina and I sold my entire one-acre allotment of tobacco. I knew this would be my last tobacco crop, and even though it was unheard of to sell it all at one time, I needed the money and I was ready to go. I received $636. I was still slightly torn as to whether I should use the money to buy a 1940 model truck for $500 or to move to Washington, DC and pursue my education. If I stayed, I could use the truck to haul items for people to earn even more money. I stood outside the used truck lot debating with myself. I thank God to this day, that the decision to move to DC prevailed. "Your father has lived his life that he has done. You have yours yet to live." I left the used truck lot, hitched a ride home, and prepared for my move to Washington, DC. The next day, I would leave the only home that I ever knew to move to Washington and start my new life.

The morning of my departure, I went to the Baynes General Store and met a guy with a pickup truck. I put my suitcase in the back. Robert Foster, another man in our community, was also on his way to DC, and we both got in the truck. Silently and nervously, we said goodbye to the only way of life we ever knew. I don't remember saying goodbye to a lot of people, but word spread that I left to pursue my dreams. Back then, when people returned from DC, they would describe it like in Exodus when the Lord said to Moses, "I will rain down bread from heaven for you." For all we knew, the streets of DC were truly paved with gold. The guy at the Baynes General Store drove us to the bus station in Danville, Virginia, and we caught the Greyhound bus. We arrived in DC around midnight.

After I left, my cousin CD, who I also considered my brother, was drafted into military service in October 1950. To think, two boys from Caswell County, North Carolina, beginning a new journey to see the world, one that was beyond our tobacco farm.

Chapter Six
My New Life in Washington, DC—High School and College

Then they said to him, "Please inquire of God to learn whether our journey will be successful." The priest said to them, "Go in peace. Your journey has the Lord's approval."
—Judges 18:5-6

The journey of a thousand miles starts with one step.
—Lao Tzu

After paying for my bus ticket and settling all the farm debts, I arrived in DC with $530 in my pocket. I moved in with my uncle and aunt, Ernest and Beulah Florence, whose house was located at 29 16th Street NE in Washington, DC. My cousin Ernest (also known as Pete) Malone, who had moved to DC the previous year, also lived with them. Pete advised me to give my money to Aunt Beulah to keep for me. This was the usual practice for boys that came from the South. So, I turned my $530 over to Aunt Beulah for safekeeping. I lived with Uncle Ernest and Aunt Beulah for three years and completed high school and two years of college. During my junior year at Howard, my living conditions in my aunt and uncle's home were not conducive for study, because so many of my homeboys from North Carolina had moved in. They were not in school, liked to party a lot, and did not understand when I had to keep the light on at night to study. I planned to move on campus; however, my Aunt Delsie heard of my plans and she insisted that I move in with her. I think she thought that living on campus was too dangerous. So, my first cousin Annie Mae, who was already living with Aunt Delsie, her husband Jule, and I reunited in their home. Mae became my sister in DC and remains to be one of my closest relatives today.

The day after arriving in DC, I was ready and eager to get into school. I arrived about a week after school started. Pete Malone, my cousin, drove me to Dunbar High School, one of the best schools in DC, but the line was too long. He said, "Let's go over to this other school I know." He took me to Armstrong High School, which we later discovered was a vocational school. Of course, there was no line and they enrolled me right away. That first month in the city was one of the loneliest of my life. I knew no one in school and missed the simplicity and comfort of living in the South; however, I quickly made friends that I still have to this day—James Fletcher who was in the class behind me and Phillip Haskins who was in my class. Armstrong High School may not have provided a great education, but it did give me lifelong friendships in a city that was still quite strange to me.

As the semester progressed, my French teacher asked me to stay after class one day. She began our conversation by saying, "You should not be in this school. If you want to go to college, this is not the right program for you." She took her concerns to the principal, but the school needed more students to bolster its enrollment, so he decided that I should stay and take general studies. I was still required to take a vocational class, so I enrolled in shop class. Phillip Haskins, my friend, was giving out the grades in shop class for the teacher. He gave me an "A" even though I didn't do any of the work.

While in high school, I began looking for a job. The first one I saw advertised in the paper was a dishwashing job at a Chinese restaurant on K Street. I walked there all the way from Northeast DC. The restaurant owner said I was overqualified because I had *not* dropped out of high school. In November 1950, Briston Williamson who was also from Caswell County just across the hill from our farm, helped me find a job at a restaurant in Silver Spring, Maryland. I worked at the restaurant from the time I was seventeen to age twenty. I graduated from high school in June 1951 and enrolled at Howard University that fall.

That summer of 1951, I joined the Army Reserve and went to Fort Campbell, Kentucky for two weeks of duty. I knew that my cousin CD was there on active duty and couldn't wait to see him. When we saw each other, it was just like old times. We were both so excited—we were like two giddy little boys back on the farm. CD was serving with the 95th Infantry, an all-black unit. The Armed Forces were in the process of integrating its troops. I was in the 80th Reserve Unit, which was already integrated. During my downtime (weekends), I would go to CD's unit, which felt much more inviting and comfortable. His unit had a party on that first weekend after my arrival. They bused in some ladies for us to dance with, but nobody danced with them. Through the years, I often teased CD about this party, because his unit was mostly gay, and they didn't even notice the women—they were too busy dancing with each other. Robert Foster, the guy who rode with me to DC from Danville, Virginia on the Greyhound bus was also stationed on that base. All three of us had left Yanceyville, North Carolina, and our travels brought us back together in Kentucky.

Back at Howard University students referred to themselves as the Captains of the Capstone—the upper echelon of historically black colleges and universities. Howard was where the Black Bourgeoisie (middle class) went to continue rising in their societal hierarchies. Those of us who were not light-skinned and had the "misfortune" of being born in the South were considered second-class citizens. The paper bag test was alive and well. If you were lighter than a paper bag, you were part of the "in crowd." The rest of us were considered unsophisticated, uncouth, and I often heard the term "country bumpkins" or comments like "they just arrived on the watermelon truck." It didn't matter to me, because it was a chance for me to prove that I could study and achieve among some of the best students in the country.

Upon arriving at Howard, I was so glad to be rid of high school truant officers chasing me, I forgot about those greater aspirations of being a scholar among scholars. Plus, someone told me that all you had to do was pass the exam to pass the class. I met a guy whose last name was Robertson. We teamed up and decided that we didn't have to go to class because we were smart enough to pass the exam. We went to Georgia Avenue and Florida Avenue and shot pool all day.

Towards the end of that first semester, I heard that there was going to be a test in science, so I went to class to take the exam. The German professor, Dr. Borwick, met me at the door and said, "Who are you?" I said, "I am Percy Baynes and I'm here to take the exam." He said, "No need. You flunked out three weeks ago." In fact, I flunked every course that semester except PE. I had a .25 grade point average. The dean called me in and said, "Unless you change your ways you will not be around to see the grass turn green."

This motivated me, perhaps even more than when my dad promised a 1940 Chevy at the end of the tobacco row. The only greater motivation was that when I decided to attend Howard, my Aunt Helen told me that my cousin Annie Mae had left Howard and transferred to Minor Teachers College to become a teacher, and so there was no way that I was going to be able to make it.

Before this source of inspiration, when I was shooting pool with Robertson and after I had been told I was flunking out, we decided to join the Air Force. We went downtown to 11th Street, the recruiter was on his way out and asked us to return the next day. Robertson went back and enlisted. I didn't go back for two reasons: (1) I could not accept failure, and (2) I had to dispel what my aunt had said about me. Robertson served for four years and I lost touch with him after that. My entire life trajectory could have changed because of a decision that I almost made while shooting pool. *But for God!*

By the end of the next quarter, I brought up my GPA to a C average. I continued to improve and became an A student by my junior year.

When I was twenty years old, I managed to get my uncle to sign a form saying that they had lost my birth certificate, so I could increase my age to twenty-one. This enabled me to take the taxi driver exam and I passed. I started driving a taxi at the age of twenty in 1953. (Incidentally, I never corrected this age discrepancy and my driver's license in 2019 still indicates that I am one year older than I really am!) That next year, Howard converted to a semester system. Working in the restaurant and driving a cab provided me with the resources to pay for my college fees.

After improving my grades and settling into the life of a real college student, I decided to pledge a fraternity. The Omega Psi Phi men on campus always impressed me as smart men who worked and partied hard. They were respected and I decided it was important to me to be among their ranks. I was asked to join the line of "Lamps" in the spring of 1953. One day, I was running late for work, when a Big Brother stopped me on the quad. He pulled an apartment key from his pocket and tried to hand it to me. He demanded that I go clean up his apartment. I tried to explain that I was on my way to work, but he insisted that this was the only work I needed to tend to. At that moment, I made the split decision to become an "Eternal Lamp"—a designation reserved for those who start pledging but never finish—or drop line. There was no choice for someone like me, with no safety net, no rich family, and no other options. I had to work so that I could stay in school and improve my life.

One summer, after I started driving the cab, I didn't have all the money needed to pay my tuition and fees at the beginning of the semester. However, there was a payment plan where you could pay a portion and settle the balance by a date certain. When that date came, I still owed $75 and the Registrar said I couldn't attend class until it was paid. I left the office not knowing how I'd make up the balance. A day or so later, I returned to tell her that I was dropping out. The Registrar then informed me that the fees had been paid in full. To this day, I don't know who paid my balance. *But for God*!

I was supposed to graduate in June of 1955 but lacked a few physical education credits. As a result, I graduated in February 1956. Since I only had to take PE, I also took other graduate classes. By the time I graduated, I had completed most of the hours that I needed for a master's degree and I was teaching in the Math Department, where I taught for a couple of semesters.

Prior to that, I worked with a professor on a grant to upgrade the skills and knowledge of math teachers from throughout the South. I remember being given the task of teaching algebra to this woman (who was old enough to be my mom) from Mississippi. I was trying to introduce the concepts and she said, "Young man, I have been in the school system for twenty-five years, and I just want a passing grade so I can get my promotion. I don't care about these theories you are talking about." Being a well-raised young man from the South, I simply responded, "Yes mam!" No amount of education can erase the level of respect for my elders that was instilled into me by my community in Sweet Gum, North Carolina.

Me in Washington DC

My Sister-Cousin Annie Mae Florence – 1953

Posing for a Picture on Kansas Avenue, NW

Cousin Annie Mae Florence - 1954

Pictured left to right: My high school graduation picture; Aunt Delsie; My Army Reserve Uniform Picture

Pictured clockwise from top left: My cousin Ernest "Pete" Malone and me; My brother John; John and our cousin W.T. Pennix; Rosa Mae Campbell at Aunt Delsie's house; My official high school graduation picture

Chapter Seven
Meeting and Marrying the Love of My Life

For this reason, a man will leave his father and mother and be united to his wife,
and the two will become one flesh.
—Ephesians 5:31

We love because it's the only true adventure.
—Langston Hughes

I remember the first day and moment that I saw Dorothy Mae Totten. There was only one high school for black students in Caswell County, and the bus went to each of the communities to pick us all up. These were not neighborhoods like the subdivisions or apartment complexes we now know in cities and suburbs. This was rural North Carolina and the various areas of the county had different names. We lived in Anderson, which included the "Sweet Gum" community. That area was most likely named after the Sweet Gum Baptist Church that we attended, and the hundreds of sweet gum trees that peppered the surrounding area.

On the first day of eighth grade in 1946, the bus picked us up in Sweet Gum and proceeded to each of the other communities. The next community was Rabbit Shuffle. Legend has it that it was named Rabbit Shuffle because the land was so poor that the rabbits could not run on it. Instead, they just shuffled along. After the bus stopped there, the funniest looking girl that I'd ever seen boarded. Her hair was parted in the middle, with two big braids that started in the front and then down toward her back. For some reason, yellow ribbons were woven through the two braids and hung down her back. I had never seen anything like it. Later, I would learn that this was Dorothy Mae Totten. They called her "Sis," because she was the only girl among five brothers (later in life I called her Dottie, which I will use throughout the rest of the book). Her class was the third room down the hall and I was in the first room. Even though I knew who she was, I don't think we actually spoke to each other that entire school year.

41

By the time we got to ninth grade, word had spread that I was good in math. I was always better at math than English. This was probably a result of not talking to people. I was raised in a quiet family. My uncle and father would work all day in the field pulling tobacco and not talk to each other. The only conversation at the dinner table was an occasional fight over the last piece of chicken. So, I found a way to express myself through numbers.

In geometry class, I noticed that other students would rush to sit next to me. The teacher always walked backward between the desks, probably to catch students cheating. Dottie and her friend Celeste Badgett were notorious for sitting behind me and looking over my shoulder to see my answers. Through math, we started talking and became good friends. As will become clear, it was math that opened many of the important doors in my life.

During high school, I started to like a young lady who lived in Buzzard's Roost, and when I could get a ride to her house, the route passed right through Rabbit Shuffle. Since Dottie had five brothers, there were always guys hanging out at their house. Her mother, who was fiercely protective of her only daughter, was adamant that she could not go anywhere with a boy until she was sixteen years old. So, I started stopping by to hang out with my new friend Dottie. She concluded that because I was so quiet, when I went to Buzzard's Roost to visit my girlfriend that we would just sit on the porch and not say anything to each other. At least when I stopped by to see her, she would talk and talk and talk. I didn't have to say a thing! She and her friends used to tell the other boys that they should be more polite and kind, like me.

Our junior year in high school was a tough one for me. Little did I know that it would be my last year living and going to school in Caswell County. That was the year that my father died. It seemed like every three years, someone important in my life died, and I didn't understand why. This was also the year that I drove the school bus. Occasionally, I'd stop at the store and buy candy to give to the other students on the bus. I always made sure that Dottie and my other friends got some of the candy first, before it was gone.

In the spring of that year, prom was approaching and I had no transportation and no date. Dottie, who was now sixteen and was allowed to date, had a boyfriend with a car, so they were going to prom together. But her girlfriend didn't have a date. Dottie's friend was going to spend the night with her and go to the prom so Dottie invited me to go with them. During the prom, her friend met an older country boy and ended up leaving with him. I was so humiliated by having to ride home with Dottie and her boyfriend, and so mad at Dottie for asking me to go to the prom with her girlfriend in the first place.

It was in late summer between our junior and senior years that I made the decision to move to DC to finish high school (see Chapter 5). I don't remember saying goodbye to a lot of people. I may have still been a little too upset or embarrassed about the prom to say goodbye to Dottie. But word spread quickly that I had left to pursue my dreams.

The first time I returned to Caswell County, after moving to DC, I went by Rabbit Shuffle to say hello to Dottie. Her father, respectfully known as "Daddy Waymond" was in his Pointer brand overalls sitting by the fireplace staring at me. Her mother left to tell Dottie that I came to visit. The next thing I knew, Dottie came running into the room and gave me a huge hug, right in front of her parents! I was mortified. In addition to being quiet, my family did not hug—especially in public. Also, I did not want to hug her back, only for her father to believe I was disrespecting his only daughter. So, not sure of what to do, I just stood there. To this day, Dottie teases me about it. She says I stood there with my arms by my sides, stiff as a statue. All I remember is that I wanted the wooden floorboards to swallow me whole, so I could just disappear!

I went back to DC and we both graduated from high school that next year. We stayed in touch—I'd tell her about my new life in DC and she would keep me abreast of what was happening in Rabbit Shuffle, Sweet Gum, and Buzzard's Roost. Dottie decided to go to Shaw University in Raleigh, North Carolina at the same time that I enrolled at Howard University in DC. She had three aunts who lived in DC, so during the summers she would catch the Trailways bus to DC to babysit their children. We saw each other quite a bit over the summers and whenever I went back home. She was still dating her high school boyfriend, and I met a few young ladies in the city, but we always enjoyed our time together.

The summer before our junior year in college, Dottie once again was in DC for the summer. On one beautiful, hot, and sweltering day, we went sightseeing downtown. No matter how much time passed between our visits, we always seemed to pick up right where we left off. She was my friend, and I realized that she let me be myself. I was starting to have feelings for her. At the end of the day, when I dropped her off at her aunt's house, I kissed Dottie for the first time. There were no words. There was no declaration. I'm sure that I surprised her, but we both knew that it was the beginning of something new.

That Christmas, I was so excited to return to Caswell County and see Dottie. I saved my money and bought her a radio for Christmas. I had it professionally wrapped so it would look even more special. In later years, I found out that my cousin Mae, who was like my sister and lived in the same house in DC, was so nosey that she secretly unwrapped the gift to see what it was. In doing so, she dropped the radio and broke off one of the knobs. She had carefully glued it back on and years later confessed her transgression to Dottie.

The following Christmas, in 1955, I proposed and gave Dottie an engagement ring. She was teaching at the time. I didn't ask Daddy Waymond for her hand in marriage because I knew he'd say no. Dottie's parents were so proud that their only daughter, a college graduate and schoolteacher, lived with them. Plus, Daddy Waymond thought she should marry her high school boyfriend Charles Blackwell. The Blackwell family owned a lot of land. To add insult to injury, Mama Bea, Dottie's mom, used to say that "Nothing good ever came out of Sweet Gum." (My community was known for its people who drank and partied too much, and often wobbled down the church aisles on Sunday mornings, still tipsy from the night before.)

We were engaged for two years. I started working in 1956 and was focused and ambitious. The engagement probably would have lasted even longer, but Dottie wrote me a letter. She was upset, tired of waiting, and asked, "When are we getting married?" When I received the letter, I thought that she may break up with me and didn't know what to do. Dottie was in North Carolina teaching and I was teaching in graduate school in DC.

That New Year's Eve, I went to New York with some cousins who also now lived in DC. Everyone used to say that there was no place else on earth to be on New Year's, than the city that never sleeps. So, we decided to check it out for ourselves. We were sitting at a bar, and I watched my drunk cousins and all the other drunk people pretending to have a good time. I knew at that moment that this was not the life for me. I was ready to go home and marry Dottie. They say that God works in mysterious ways, but I never knew that He would literally pluck you right out of a juke joint.

As soon as I had the chance, I went back to Rabbit Shuffle to see Dottie and her family. When I walked into their house, there was Daddy Waymond sitting by the fireplace with his overalls and jacket. I said, "Mr. Totten, Dottie and I have decided to get married." Mama Bea was so upset that she left the room. Dottie was probably so nervous that she too left the room, leaving us two men to hash it out.

Daddy Waymond said, "Why do you have to do it so soon?" I thought to myself, my goodness, it has been two years! Knowing that this argument would not go well, I said, "I have orders to report to the Army and we want to get married before I leave." His only response was, "You ought to wait."

In February 1957. Dottie was working in Princeton, North Carolina (Johnson County). My friend Clemon Bigelow and I drove down Highway 301 and picked her up, and we then drove to Caswell County arriving on a Friday. Clemon came along to serve as a witness (plus, he just liked to take road trips). We dropped Dottie at her parents' house. I got the marriage license in Graham, North Carolina. Saturday morning, we picked Dottie up and the three of us went to Doc Howard's house. We left Daddy Waymond and Mama Bea who were both very sad. After our marriage, Aunt Mae, Mama Bea's sister convinced Mama Bea that Dottie had a wonderful husband. Subsequently, Dottie's parents gave us a celebration party in their home.

Doc Howard was a produce farmer and served as a Baptist preacher for a local congregation. When we pulled up to his house, he was outside plowing his garden with his mule. I asked him if he would marry us and he said that we should return that evening and he would conduct the ceremony. Later that evening, Dottie and I exchanged our marriage vows in Doc Howard's living room. In 1957, there were no motels or hotels where black people could stay due to segregation and Jim Crow laws. There was one old motel, but it was rundown and used mainly by prostitutes and their customers. So that night, we ended up staying with my oldest sister Catherine and her husband Allison. When we woke up the next morning, no one was home. There was a note taped to the fridge that said, "There's bacon and eggs in the fridge—help yourself."

This was the beginning of a sixty-two-year marriage to the love of my lifetime. The little girl with yellow ribbons in her hair, Dorothy Mae Totten, honored me by becoming Dorothy Totten Baynes.

Dorothy "Sis" Totten in Rabbit Shuffle

Dorothy Mae Totten 1949

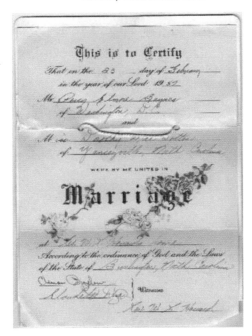

Our Marriage Certificate

Chapter Eight
The Early Years—Our Summer in Oklahoma

And over all these virtues put on love, which binds them all together in perfect unity.
—Colossians 3:14

Lots of people want to ride with you in the limo, but what you want is someone who will take the bus with you when the limo breaks down.
—Oprah Winfrey

During the Korean War, I was still a student at Howard University. I joined the Air Force ROTC from 1951 to 1952, with hopes of becoming a pilot. For advanced ROTC you had to score high on an examination to determine your fitness. I went to Boiling Air Force Base, and unfortunately discovered that I did not have 20/20 vision and therefore could not qualify as a pilot. Undeterred, I returned to campus and joined the Army ROTC program instead. I graduated from Howard in February 1956 and received a commission as a second Lieutenant in the Army ROTC. Also in 1956, the Reserve Act of 1956 was enacted by Congress, which allowed military servicemen to serve six months of active duty and 7.5 years in the Reserves. I elected to take this route and was called into active duty in March 1957. Originally, I was supposed to go to Fort Bliss in Texas to enroll in Missile School. Instead, I was assigned to Ft. SILL in Oklahoma for my six months of active duty. Dottie and I were married on February 23rd and I had to report to Oklahoma on March 6th for Officers Basic Training.

Reporting to Oklahoma

I purchased my first car in November of 1956. It was a red and black hardtop convertible that cost me $2300, which I spread out into monthly payments over two years. Four months later, I decided to leave the car with Dottie while I was in Oklahoma. Uncle Ernest told me that I had clearly lost my mind, but I was in love, this was my wife, and she needed transportation. So, I drove the car to North Carolina, left it with Dottie and caught the train to Oklahoma.

The train departed from Raleigh, North Carolina, traveled through Mississippi, and arrived in Memphis Tennessee, where I disembarked to wait for another train. I was hungry and found a local restaurant. I sat at the counter, looked over the menu, and decided on a tuna sandwich. When a black waitress walked up, I thought she was going to take my order. Instead, she leaned over and whispered that she could not serve me at the counter.

As I was traveling to Oklahoma to serve my country, the good citizens of Montgomery, Alabama, led by the charismatic and brilliant young preacher, Martin Luther King, Jr., were starting their third month of a bus boycott to put an end to Jim Crow segregation practices. *Brown v. Board of Education* had legally desegregated schools just two years before in 1954. The Civil Rights Movement was in full swing. Yet, Memphis and other cities found ways to circumvent the new laws. It was in 1956 that the Southern Manifesto Bill, opposing racial integration in public places, was signed by 101 Senators and Congressmen, all from Southern states. I was aware that all this was happening and followed it closely, but it never occurred to me that I'd be traveling on a train that would take me through many of the cities that were ground zero for the resistance and activism.

Within a few minutes of hearing the young waitress's words, it hit me that my presence at the counter was not welcome in Memphis, Tennessee because of the color of my skin. I turned to her and said, "I'm tired. I have been traveling all night. Uncle Sam called me into military service, and I am not moving from this seat." She looked as though she wanted to cry. She then left quickly to get her manager, probably hoping that she would not lose her job. The manager, a white man, came over to me. Once he learned that I was on my way to Fort Sill for basic training, he turned to the young black waitress and said, "Serve him."

I sat there and endured the scowls and stares from the other white patrons while eating the best tuna sandwich I'd ever had. The tuna, mixed with mayonnaise and resistance brought joy to my tongue, and satisfaction to my soul. I guess, in my own way, I helped to integrate the lunch counters in Memphis, Tennessee. This was four years before the infamous lunch counter sit-ins that occurred in 1960 in Greensboro, North Carolina. I finished my lunch and boarded the train to Oklahoma.

While I was enrolled in the Field Artillery Basic Training School for Officers, Dottie continued to teach in North Carolina. One day, she drove our car to my sister Catherine's house to give her daughter Jean a doll. When she opened the passenger door to get the doll, and in her excitement, did not completely close the door before entering the house. On her way home, that same door flew open, and as she reached over to close it, she ran the car off the road and into a ditch. I later discovered that her cousin's husband, Oscar Wright, a local mechanic, tried to bang out the dents as much as possible. Uncle Ernest had been right, but not because I lost my mind in letting Dottie keep the car. I realized that the love I felt for my new wife outweighed the importance that I had once placed on things like a car. In a quick daydream, I saw Dottie standing at the end of the row of tobacco, and all I could do was smile.

After basic training, we were given a fifteen-day leave to go home. It was June, and Dottie and I went to DC and stayed with Aunt Delsie for a few days, before driving to Oklahoma together for the summer. By the time we reached Columbus, Ohio, I was getting tired. We did not stop at any hotels because segregation and discriminatory practices were alive and real. Dottie volunteered to drive, and although the driving-in-the-ditch incident was still very fresh, I agreed. She took over the wheel and I settled into the passenger seat and went to sleep. At some point, I heard her sweet voice calmly saying, "Percy, what should I do?" As I woke up, I looked to my right and saw the huge tires of a tractor trailer. I then looked to my left and saw the wheels of another tractor trailer. We were sandwiched between two eighteen-wheeler trucks, all of us going seventy miles per hour.

In a very quiet and feigned relaxed tone, I said, "Slow down." She did. As the trucks pulled away, I said, "Now, move to the right lane." She did. Finally, out of danger, I said, "Why don't you pull off the road?" After reaching the safety of the shoulder, I turned to the love of my life and said, "You are not driving anymore!" After that, I drove straight through to Oklahoma, and in our sixty-two years of marriage, I don't remember many times that Dottie drove when I was in the car.

Prior to our trip to Oklahoma, I had rented an apartment and furniture to make sure that Dottie was comfortable for the summer. It was supposed to be all set up when we arrived. As we drove up to the apartment, I was anxious to show off our new place. When we opened the door, the apartment was completely empty! I tried to hide my disappointment and Dottie was a real trooper. We checked into the Officer's Club for a couple of nights. After we maxed out our time there, we stayed with my friend Gordon and his wife and slept on their couch until our apartment was ready.

Our first summer as husband and wife was very exciting in the Oklahoma dust belt. On weekends we would go up to Mount Scott, located in the Wichita Mountains near the Fort Sill Military Reservation. We visited other interesting places in and around Lawton, Oklahoma. Native Americans always fascinated me. Everyone in Sweet Gum used to say that my grandmother had a lot of Native American blood. Her hair was jet black, straight, and long. She used to wear it wrapped up in a neat bun on the back of her head. Her cheekbones were strong and sat high on her face, framing a keen nose and full lips.

Oklahoma has the second largest population of Native Americans in the country and is home to thirty-nine different tribes. After living in Oklahoma for six months, I left with a greater understanding of the struggles of the Apache, Caddo, and Cherokee tribes.

At the end of our summer in Oklahoma, I arranged for Dottie to fly home. She had insisted on leaving because she'd signed a teaching contract for the upcoming school year. She could have broken the contract, but for Dottie, her word was her bond, so she had to fulfill her commitment. This was one of the many things that I love about my wife—her integrity was unflappable.

The flight from Oklahoma to North Carolina was not long, but it was the first time that Dottie had ever been on an airplane. She was so scared! I drove her to the airport and as we walked hand in hand through the terminal, I could literally feel her shaking. As we passed a kiosk advertising flight insurance, Dottie turned to me and jokingly said, "Look Percy, you can get flight insurance in case my plane crashes."

Not catching the joke, I responded, "That's a great idea!" So, right there in front of my nerve-wracked wife, I purchased an insurance policy on her life. This was when I first realized that I couldn't read Dottie's mind. Her insurance suggestion had been made from jest and a fear of flying. My response, although based on logic and practicality, completely disregarded Dottie's fear and feelings. This was the first of many lessons in our life together that I learned more about Dottie and realized more about myself.

Dottie outside our home in Oklahoma and me as a young reserve officer

Chapter Nine
Our Spiritual Home and Family:
First Baptist Church of Washington, DC

*Like newborn babies, crave pure spiritual milk, so that by it you may grow up
in your salvation, now that you have tasted that the Lord is good.*
—1 Peter 2-3

*The secret of my success? It is simple. It is found in the Bible: In all thy ways
acknowledge Him and He shall direct thy paths.*
—George Washington Carver

Dottie and I both grew up at tending churches in Caswell
County, North Carolina. Her family attended Blackwell Missionary
Baptist Church and as aforementioned my family attended Sweet
Gum Grove Missionary Baptist Church. In fact, I cannot recall
anyone I knew growing up who did not attend church. It was as
much a part of our lives as eating and breathing. However, even
though I did not miss a Sunday at church as a child, and even
after my burning bush moment following my father's death, when
I arrived in DC, I had stopped attending church. This may have
been in part because we were required to attend services at
Howard University's Rankin Memorial Chapel every Thursday. I
paid Aunt Delsie rent to stay in her home, and she did not go out
of her way to tend to my spiritual growth. Occasionally, Uncle
Ernest or Aunt Fanny would invite me to an event at their
churches. Typically, however, I spent Sundays working in
restaurants and eventually driving my cab. Even after Dottie and
I got married, it took me a decade to return to church. I no
longer believed that the church was the vehicle for understanding
my purpose.

But Dottie felt differently. I don't think there was ever a Sunday
that she missed going to church. She started attending services
at First Baptist Church, in Northwest Washington, DC with my
cousin Mae. After we had children, she and Mae took them to
church and Sunday school without fail. I usually stayed home and

washed my car, only attending occasionally. I distinctly remember the day that catapulted my desire to learn and grow spiritually.

In 1961, I left David Taylor Model Base, Department of Navy, and started working at Goddard Space Center (National Aeronautics and Space Administration [NASA]). Through my work at NASA, my understanding and appreciation for the universe expanded exponentially. One Sunday, after church, I had an interesting discussion with Minister Frank Tucker, the Youth Minister of the First Baptist Church in DC. The discussion centered on our scientific broadening perspective of the Earth. If we no longer saw the world as flat, how might that change our perspective from a biblical perspective? The church pastor, Reverend R. Levell Tucker, Minister Frank Tucker's uncle, then got me involved in his Sunday school class. I was so excited about the round Earth - no longer believed to have four corners - and our classes each Sunday fascinated me. As a result of my enthusiasm, he asked me to teach the class in 1963 on a Sunday when he could not make it. It turns out that due to illness and eventually retirement, he never returned. I would go on to teach that Sunday school class from 1963 until we moved back to North Carolina in 2011.

Studying and preparing to teach Sunday school gave me a greater appreciation for the whole biblical story. I often liked to contrast the scientific approach with the biblical creation. Somehow, within my own mind, I was able to resolve the discrepancies. I came to believe that there truly was a spiritual concern at play. I began to realize that God is a Spirit, and we should worship him in spirit and in truth. I grew to recognize that the truth is found in the Bible. One worships God in spirit and not in the physical being. Throughout my life, I always believed that God was a big man with human qualities, judging me for my sins. In some ways, I felt as though God had been punishing me since the day my mother died when I was three years old.

When I moved to DC, I was determined to prove that God did not exist. I could not believe with all the death and loss in my life that God's existence could be real. How could he have allowed these terrible things to happen as a real and benevolent God? I decided that math could provide the answer. The great mathematician Pascal started an equation that he was unable to complete. As a student at Howard, I decided to pick up where he left off, and finish it. I eventually developed an ill-defined equation and finally realized that my struggle was really all about faith. From that day that I laid in the gully on the farm and heard the voice speaking to me, I knew in my heart that there was a God.

We moved to California in 1972, and I began practicing devotions every morning. Dottie found a jar of scriptures written on pieces of paper and the kids took turns pulling and reading them before saying grace at dinner. We would drive into Los Angeles every Sunday to attend a black church. I came to understand that my faith is strengthened when I take the time to study and commune with God first thing in the morning.

So, each morning I thank God for providing for me rest during the night and allowing me to get up in the morning. I then ask Him what He wants me to do. I ask Him to grant me wisdom, knowledge, and understanding so that I can do those things that He has planned for me. Then I am ready to go forward with another day. Through faith, I have come to understand that everything I am able to accomplish is through His grace and mercy.

Daily study and meditation have also allowed me to gain a greater appreciation of the plan that God has for each one of us. The main goal in life is to discover our purpose and dedicate ourselves to it, knowing that it is God's plan and we are working to glorify Him. Learning this truth has changed my life. I wanted my children to grow up in this truth and Dottie and I took them to Sunday school and church every Sunday without fail.

When we moved back to Maryland, First Baptist Church was once again our spiritual home and the congregants became our extended family. Together, with this upstanding group of faithful black people, we loved and helped raise one another's children. We taught them vital lessons about black history, which were not taught in public schools. It was at the First Baptist Church that our sons Percival and Steve first experienced the Boy Scouts. It was there that our daughter Anita formed some of her closest friendships. First Baptist gave our other daughter Karen an opportunity to develop her skills in public speaking through oratory contests and the choral speakers. Each of our children would all find their own way to Christ and each one was baptized in our church.

The friendships that Dottie and I formed were powerful beyond measure, and together we all experienced and supported each other through the joys and sorrows of life. I was blessed to serve on the Deacon Board, the Board of Trustees, and the Finance Committee. Deacon Ralph Peters, a leader in his own right, was

Chairman of the Board when I joined, and taught each of us how to be strong men of service for Christ. Whether we were serving communion for the sick and shut-ins or helping set up tables at the annual Sunday school picnics that took place in various parks in the city, including Rock Creek Park, we developed a fellowship with one another that has lasted for decades.

The Men's Choir, under the leadership of Robert Parker, fed my soul in ways I never imagined. It took me back to those hot sweltering Sundays in Sweet Gum. It was Mrs. Glasby and Bill Slade who provided comic relief when tensions began to flare with the Board of Trustees. During the 1980s, the crack epidemic led to increasing crime rates in the city. One Wednesday, we were having a Trustee meeting in the Senior Center when an armed robber entered and made all of us lay down on the floor. As he brandished his gun, he had each of us empty our pockets and hand over our wallets and jewelry. After he left and we knew that we were safe, I'll never forget Trustee Lawrence boasting that he still had money hidden in his underwear. I thought he was willing to risk our lives for a few dollars. Later, we would all laugh about it together. The church was full of characters that enriched our lives, the lives of our children, and the community of Northwest Washington, DC.

First Baptist Church of Washington, DC

The Sanctuary during Christmas

First Baptist Church Deacon Board

Chairman of Deacon Board

Deacon Percy Baynes

Percival in the Church Boy Scouts Troop

Chapter Ten
Navigating the Workforce
and the Civil Rights Movement

Whatever you do, work at it with all your heart, as working for the Lord, not for human masters.
—Colossians 3:23

*Education is the passport to the future, for tomorrow belongs to those who prepare
for it today.*
—Malcom X

While still a student at Howard, there was a physics professor, Dr. Branson, who was one of my mentors. I went to his office one day and I told him I needed a real job to earn some money. He tried to talk me into staying in school and the merits of earning more degrees. Just to satisfy him, I applied to a doctoral program at Ohio State University and got accepted. I decided to turn it down and instead went to work at David Taylor Model Base, Department of the Navy in 1956.

David Taylor Model Basin

When I began working at the David Taylor Model Basin, in Bethesda, Maryland, my job entailed writing programs to determine the vibration of ships in the water. I was a GS-5 earning $4480 per year. My direct supervisor was Dr. Elizabeth Cuthill, who was famous for writing the Cuthill Code for nuclear reactors. We worked on one of the earliest computers, the UNIVAC 1. (*The fifth machine built for the U.S. Atomic Energy Commission was used by CBS to predict the results of the 1952 presidential election of Eisenhower. We worked on the sixth machine.*)

There was a larger computer at the U.S. Naval base in Dahlgren, Virginia that we also used to write code. Elizabeth Cuthill, Maxine Jackson, and I drove 72 miles into this small rural, predominantly white community every time we needed to access the computer for our work. Elizabeth was white with a long ponytail and Maxine was black. (It is interesting to note that Maxine graduated from Shaw University a year before Dottie.) The Dahlgren community was segregated and there were no restaurants that would serve Maxine or me. So, we ate in the Navy's cafeteria which was racially integrated but segregated by gender. So, I still could not eat with them. During one of our trips to Dahlgren, Elizabeth, who always drove, was talking so much that she missed a turn and we ended up right in the middle of a drive-in movie theater. Never a dull day!

National Aeronautics and Space Administration (NASA)

In 1961, NASA was looking for mathematicians. I applied and was offered a job and went to work at Goddard Space Flight Center in Greenbelt, Maryland, where I stayed for 15 years. I was heading up a programming section and it was there that I met and hired Bill Slade, who became one of my closest friends. We were exactly 10 years apart, both born on May 1st, and both from rural North Carolina. Together at NASA, we developed code to track the orbit of the unmanned spacecraft.

My work at NASA was fascinating and provided me with the opportunity to delve more deeply into my passion for mathematics. I joined the organization during an extraordinary time in the history of America's space program and a notable time in the history of the Civil Rights Movement. During the same year that I joined NASA, the Freedom Riders, groups of black and white Civil Rights activists took buses from DC to the South to test a Supreme Court ruling that segregation of interstate transportation facilities (including bus stations) was unconstitutional. Knowing that bus terminals in the South still had "whites only" restrooms and lunch counters, the Freedom Riders attempted to use them and were met with violence, including the bombing of a bus outside of Aniston, Alabama. The world was beginning to take note. President John F. Kennedy also gave his famous Man-on-the-Moon-by-the-End-of-the-Decade speech. During this time, the federal government was not even integrated. NASA was trying to lead the world in space exploration, but still had separate bathrooms for black and white employees. In 1961, Kennedy signed an Executive Order requiring federal agencies to hire more minority employees and contractors.

Living in Washington, DC, the Civil Rights Movement was an integral part of our lives. Even though I was working long hours and we now had two children, I still attended meetings, and supported the cause. The March on Washington for Jobs and Freedom took place on August 28, 1963, and I was determined to go. Martin Luther King, Jr. and all the other leaders were calling for us to congregate on the National Mall in DC. Dottie was frightened about the potential violence that might take place and begged me not to go. But my soul and spirit would not allow me to stay home. If I close my eyes, I can still hear Mahalia Jackson singing and later saying, "Tell 'em about the dream Martin." I left the National Mall that day knowing that our country would never be the same—my heart was full of hope and belief that our children would have endless opportunities. In less than a month, that hope would be tested beyond measure, when four little girls died after segregationists bombed the 16th Street Baptist Church in Birmingham, Alabama. The nation continued mourning in November of that same year when President John F. Kennedy was shot and killed in Dallas, Texas.

Everyone remembers where they were on those devastating days. Dottie and I were at church with our two children on the day the four girls were killed in Birmingham. President Kennedy was murdered on Friday, November 22, 1963. I was working at Goddard when we received the news that he had been shot. We gathered around a television in the break room and witnessed history as Walter Cronkite choked back tears and announced to the nation that the president was dead. Some people cried; others walked away in stunned silence. I just remember thinking, "All the planning and testing we have done, and the president will not be able to witness his vision and mandate for us to land men on the moon and return to Earth within this decade."

The Civil Rights Act was passed and signed into law in 1964, followed by the Voting Rights Act of 1965. For black families living in DC and many of us working in the federal government, we thought we had arrived. The law was finally on our side. We soon began to understand and witness the increased levels of resistance against the enforcement of the new laws, including violence. The decade of murder continued with Malcom X's assassination in February of 1965.

On Thursday, April 4, 1968, at 6 pm, Dr. King was shot in Memphis, Tennessee. By 8 pm, news of his death hit the airwaves in and around the DC area. I was working late at Goddard that night, when we received the word. My mind began reeling. "How could this happen? He was such a man of faith and peace!" I didn't have time to fully explore my emotions at that moment—I knew that the city would erupt in anger and rioting. All I could think of was Dottie at home alone with our four children, the youngest of which was under the age of one.

I ran out of the building, jumped into my car, and headed back into DC to be with my family. The radio confirmed my greatest fear; as night settled over the city, smoke began to rise from the blazes that were being deliberately set by frustrated and angry Washingtonians. The police were out in full force, fully armed and deploying tear gas in an attempt to disperse the inflamed crowds. I continued driving into the city, praying that Dottie and the kids were okay. There was literally a hazy fog from the ash and tear gas permeating the air. Other than my moment in the gully after my father's death, I cannot remember praying with more deliberateness and fervor.

As I neared Riggs Park in Northeast DC, a police barricade blocked the intersection. They were not allowing anyone to pass. I rolled down my window and tried to plead with the officer to let me through so that I could ensure my family's safety. It took several attempts, I showed him my driver's license with our street address, I displayed my NASA identification badge, and finally pictures of our children from my wallet. I finally told the officer that I was a man of faith and had been praying to God for my family's safety. The police officer eventually believed that I wasn't trying to enter the city to loot and destroy property, and relented, letting me pass through the barricade. When I reached our row house on 12th Street, everyone was safe and sound. For the next four days, the city continued to burn with over 1000 separate fires, 7600 people were arrested, 9000 businesses were destroyed, and 13 people lost their lives, including a 15-year-old boy whose remains would not be discovered for another three years. It was one of the worst riots in the history of our country. We stayed at home, hunkered down, praying and believing that God would deliver our family and our community. That Sunday, determined to return our city back to some sense of normalcy, we along with thousands of other DC residents attended church for Palm Sunday. It was reported that there were over 12,000 National Guard members and troops from the 82nd Airborne patrolling the city or on route to the city that Sunday. Not exactly what anyone would expect in preparation for Easter. The world was changing as rapidly as our advances in developing a new frontier in space. As a young black man, husband, father, and son of God, I was trying to find my footing in the community and at work.

In 1972, Melba Roy, who was a supervising mathematician, told me that NASA was looking for someone to join the President's Interchange Program (PIP). I interviewed at Headquarters and was accepted into the program.

Presidential Interchange Program

The Presidential Interchange Program (PIP) started in 1970 under an Executive Order that was signed by President Lyndon B. Johnson. The order authorized one-year exchanges of "promising young executives" between the government and the private sector. The civil servants who worked for business were paid by the companies and the businessmen were paid by the government agencies for which they worked.

Out of the 35 candidates selected for the PIP in 1972, only two of us were black. The selection process involved interviewing with various companies in the private sector to determine if there was a suitable match for each participant's background and experience.

Prior to beginning the initial assignment, we also met and interviewed with many Congressmen and White House officials. One of these interviews still stands out. It was with Senator William Fulbright from Arkansas. The Fulbright Scholarship, one of the most competitive and prestigious fellowships in the world, was named after Senator Fulbright, the sponsor of the bill. The night before our meeting, I agonized over the interview, worried that I'd be unnerved by this globally important man. I then thought that he puts his pants on the same way that I do, so we can simply talk man to man. This helped me let down my guard and release my nervousness, and it was a wonderful experience that I will always remember.

I also interviewed with two corporations: Continental Can in New York and Rockwell International in California. I was offered a position with Continental Can, but New York did not seem like it would be the best place for my family. Even though the program was only for one year, by 1972, Dottie and I had four children. Together, we made the decision that wherever I took a position, our entire family would go. We looked at it as an adventure for all of us. I later interviewed with and was selected by the aerospace company, Rockwell International, to work in Downey, California.

Prior to reporting to work, they offered Dottie and me an advance trip to find a house. After a few days of searching, we found a house in Palos Verdes, California, 26 miles from work, but in a safe and comfortable neighborhood with great schools for the kids. The house was a three-bedroom rambler, with a slight view of the Pacific Ocean, a nice yard, and a garage. Occasionally, the kids got a kick out of seeing wild peacocks from the patio.

It turned out to be ideal. The house was within walking distance of Redondo Beach. We moved to California in November 1972, two days before the election of President Richard Nixon on November 4th. Somehow, we arrived before our furniture and belongings, which were being transported by Bekins Moving Company (I remember this, because to this day, I still find Bekins stickers on the bottom of some of our furniture). As a result, our first days living in California, were in a motel room—all six of us— Dottie, the four children, and me. (Thinking back, I guess I could have sprung for two rooms, but that one room was about the size of my birth home, so I was just fine.) This was the beginning of a life-altering and memorable year. Two days later, the furniture arrived, and we moved into our Palos Verdes home away from home. Dottie was willing to leave her family, her friends, and her job to move across the country with our four children. Her sacrifices, love, and support would continue to amaze me throughout our life and marriage. My wife was a woman of great faith!

On the first day that I reported for work at Rockwell in Downy, it rained so much it seemed like a monsoon! By the time I parked my car and walked to the office entrance, the water was almost up to my knees. I remember thinking, "Lord, are you trying to tell me something?" Once inside, I was ushered to what I thought would be my office. I did not realize that Rockwell had a "Bank of America"-style office configuration; just one big room full of desks, so that heads were looking at the back of heads. There must have been a sea of 60 people in this one area, which I quickly noted only included one or two black or brown faces, inclusive of my own. Supervisors and managers had their own offices.

One guy, who considered himself the white rebel (more like a white supremacist) took it upon himself to prevent black employees from becoming supervisors. He constantly tried to do things to harass me. It was always subtle, yet targeted. For example, when I'd make suggestions, he'd say, "I have been working here for a long time and we don't do it that way."

My response, always direct and invisible of anger, "Well, you have not been working on this project, so we will do it this way."

After working at Rockwell for one week, I received a call from Willard Rockwell, Chairman of the Board. He was also on the Board of Directors for the Presidential Interchange Program. Mr. Rockwell's office was located at the airport and he wanted to meet me. I went to meet him and his office was the largest one I had ever seen. He greeted me and wanted to know how things were going since joining the Rockwell family. I told him that things were going well, but that I had anticipated more privacy in my work environment. He said, "We will fix that!" By the time I returned to the office in Downey, they had carved out a private office for me, which came with a new title—Manager of Software Requirements. Rockwell won the contract to build the Orbiter for the Space Shuttle, so the position was a perfect match for my knowledge and experience at NASA.

During my year with Rockwell, I pulled together many of the subcontractors to develop the onboard guidance and computer software for the onboard computers, which included four computers that had to operate in sync and communicate while simultaneously communicating with another backup computer.

Also during that year, I initiated a contract for Rockwell with Draper Lab in Massachusetts to develop HAL (Higher-Order Language) to write the software for the onboard computers. My team and I traveled to Cambridge, Massachusetts to oversee the contract, as well as to the Massachusetts Institute of Technology (MIT) campus to monitor the brilliant researchers that were developing the flight software for guidance, navigation, and control (GNC) algorithms. One of the interesting things about working with top-notch scientists at MIT was that they were so brilliant, they'd constantly develop "better" ways of doing things. Unfortunately, this meant that when we visited every two weeks for status reports, their "better" ways of doing things were constantly delaying the project. Once we realized that we were not making much progress, we baselined an approach and made them stick to it in order to keep the program moving forward. At Cambridge, the development of HAL went very well and was extremely successful. In some ways, I was getting that PhD education that I had passed up. I often wondered if the nation's top scientific minds assigned to our project had any idea that I grew up on a tobacco farm in the rural South. God truly does have a sense of humor!

In addition to going to Massachusetts, I also traveled to Houston, Texas, where the NASA Program Office responsible for Orbiter development was located (Manned Space Flight Center). My first visit was in August, and having never been to Houston in the summertime, I was unaware of how hot, humid, and sticky weather could affect a person's clothes. I had purchased what I thought was a nice suit at a great price. By the time I walked from the car to the office, my pants had drawn up above my shoe tops! The weather was so oppressive that a fellow coworker that traveled with me from California, developed a collapsed lung and was hospitalized. After that trip, I increased the price and quality of my suits to withstand any kind of weather. (I must have done a pretty good job, because I still wear some of those suits to this day!)

Another time in Houston, we were in a conference room having a spirited discussion about the degree of accuracy needed for algorithms. There was one big guy who worked for the government in Houston. He stood up and said, "We are all white and free, why can't we make a decision."

Of course, I was the only black person in the room. As I felt eyes nervously looking my way, I responded, "Phil, I understand what you are saying, because I was walking down the street in Houston the other day and someone tried to buy me." The entire room erupted in laughter and Phil and I went on to be close colleagues. Sometimes you have to be able to defuse racial tension in order to get work done. Where I found the strength to answer without anger, I do not know. I guess, with the help of God. I had truly evolved.

There were many other times like this when I surprised myself. A boy once so full of anger in Caswell County, North Carolina, now went toe to toe with a room full of white men, using only my intellect and faith in God.

Before the end of our year, there was one week when all PIP participants, government, and industry traveled together to London, England. The purpose of the trip was to meet and shadow government officials in Great Britain in order to understand how they conducted business—protocol, processes, and so on. It was enjoyable and meaningful, in that my perspective had now moved beyond the United States.

Return to NASA

My year at Rockwell was fruitful. Before I left, Mr. Rockwell offered to hire me for any position that I wanted if I would stay in California and continue working with his team. Lockheed also expressed an interest in hiring me, and I interviewed with them as well. I had learned so much and felt I'd also contributed a great deal. There was also something about the West Coast environment that I really loved. But in the end, I missed the four seasons, and I had promised Dottie that our adventure would only last a year. We were far from our families and I wanted to go back to my *big government job*.

We moved back into our house in Maryland, and I returned to Goddard Space Flight Center to my previously held GS-14 grade level position. Within a month, I received a promotion to Manager of Onboard Orbiter Software, a GS-15 position located at NASA Headquarters in Southwest DC. It seemed that after my year in California, I was the most knowledgeable person at NASA Headquarters about the costly work being done at Rockwell. The Administration wanted to stay abreast of what was going on with the development of the Orbiter vehicle. I conducted workshops for the senior managers of NASA on how to write software. Even the Director of the Space Shuttle Program attended my sessions. He was under a great amount of pressure and had to be able to clearly articulate how federal dollars were being spent. I served in this position until 1980, when they expanded the office and created an Avionics Branch to focus on the onboard avionics.

They advertised the new position at the Senior Executive Level (SES). So, I applied thinking that my unique experience during my PIP assignment at Rockwell was a great advantage. There were other engineers who also applied. I was selected and appointed to the position of Chief of the Avionics Branch at NASA Headquarters. Later, I was told that one of the technical guys on the selection committee, who I knew casually, really pushed for me when the panel argued on behalf of a candidate from Houston. He insisted that I was the most qualified. Later, the position of Executive Director of the Orbiter Division was created, and I was selected as a lateral transfer. This was the position I held until my retirement from NASA in 1984.

As the Executive Director of the Orbiter Division, I was more visible than I preferred. I was truly an introvert. Despite my broadening perspective and extraordinary experiences, I still didn't like to socialize with a lot of people or talk unless I truly had something to say. Prior to being selected for the SES position, I was profiled in an *Ebony Magazine* article highlighting blacks in federal government. What meant more to me than anything though was how proud Dottie was about the article. While I was building my career and trying to make a difference in the world, she was succeeding too as a teacher and as the mother of our four growing children. I was proud of her too. We were in this life together.

Memorable Moments at NASA

The First Successful Launch

In April of 1981, we flew to Kennedy Space Flight Center in Cape Canaveral, Florida for the first Space Shuttle flight. Space Shuttle *Columbia* was the world's first reusable aircraft to carry humans into orbit. I will never forget hearing the words after the countdown, "And we have liftoff, liftoff of America's first space shuttle!" This was followed by, "The shuttle has cleared the tower." Cheers, applause, and high fives erupted throughout the control room. After so many years in the making; however, this was just the first part of the journey. We also had to ensure that the Orbiter was able to reenter the Earth's atmosphere and bring the astronauts safely back to Kennedy Space Center, Florida two days later. Sure enough, after the successful launch on April 12th, the Orbiter safely returned on April 14th, marking the beginning of a storied 30 years of missions. On that day in April 1981, we celebrated with each other and headed back to DC. We landed back at Reagan National Airport and people were lined up as we disembarked from the NASA plane loudly cheering, holding signs, and saying thank you for making this happen. The entire country witnessed the next great step in our space program. At that moment, I was overwhelmed by the difference our work was making in the world.

Being in the Control Room

In my role as the Executive Director of the Orbiter Division, I attended all the launches. During the launch process, each element manager takes their position in the control room manning a console. I manned the console for the Orbiter, ensuring that all the performance parameters stayed within limits. On occasion, a countdown was stopped for various reasons.

The control room was a glass-enclosed room in the middle of the control center. During one launch, I noticed a small black man staring through the glass directly at me. He stood out because there were not many black people in the room during the launch and he was the darkest black man I had ever seen. We shut down the launch to investigate some out of limit performance parameters. Those parameters were not within my purview. My curiosity got the best of me, and I went out to find out why this striking man was staring at me. As I approached to shake his hand, he said to me, "I have been praying all my life. I never thought I would see a black man in the control room." It made me think of when they took Jesus to be blessed. And the priest said, I can now go see the Lord. I simply said to the man, "Bless you." It turned out that he was a custodian at Kennedy Space Flight Center, and he allowed me to buy him breakfast in the cafeteria. My presence in that control room made him so happy, and his fortitude and faith made me so proud. At that moment, he represented all the strong men who had made my journey possible. My father and grandfather left the earth too soon, but their spirits lived within me. We, my ancestors, and this man who honored me by having breakfast with me, all sat in that control room. I never took it for granted again.

Leaving NASA

The former director of the Space Shuttle Program left NASA and began working for a company in the private sector. He was recruiting and wanted to know if I had any recommendations for a software engineering position. I asked him to tell me more about the job. After he described it, something made me say, "I might be interested."

He smiled broadly and said, "Seriously!" I responded, "Yes." He then asked for my resume. I hesitated because at that point in time, I was the highest-ranking black person working in a technical discipline at NASA. The role would give me the opportunity to mentor other young black professionals and help them navigate the workforce in the same way that others helped me. I gave him my resume anyway, and he called me within a week to schedule the interview. I thought, "What have I done?" And I accepted the interview with Vitro Corporation. Although I had no intention of accepting the job if it was offered. During my interview, however, I was really impressed with the managers. There was also a Senior Vice President who had a large corner office that seemed bigger than my house! I walked in not knowing if we'd have anything in common to discuss when I spotted a Bible on his desk. Knowing that he was a man of faith put me at ease and we had an incredible conversation. I met with several other vice presidents and the president, and then returned to NASA. They called me in two days and made me an offer I could not refuse. I worked at Vitro for 10 years, serving as the Director of Software Engineering and Vice President of Software Engineering.

The Shuttle Disaster

In 1986, two years after I left NASA, the world watched as the Space Shuttle exploded shortly after launch. The Lord moved me out before this disaster that would forever change the course of our nation's space program. I knew all the astronauts onboard that day. The one that I remember the most was a young black astronaut named Ronald McNair. While I didn't work with him directly, I had admired him from afar. I was later asked to return to NASA as an advisor and had the opportunity to meet McNair's lovely wife. When the second Space Shuttle Orbiter exploded on its way back into the Earth's atmosphere, I was a part of the team (NASA Advisory Team) that reviewed the debris to help to determine the cause.

After retiring from Vitro in 1994, I consulted with Anteon and later took a position there as Director of Technology for three years. While working at Anteon, I was asked to join the NASA Advisory Group to conduct ongoing reviews of the International Space Station. The Space Station is a joint project between the United States and Russia. The reviews required frequent trips to Moscow and Houston, Texas. While I have never been a heavy drinker, the amount of vodka consumed by our Russian colleagues was obscene. They would start early in the morning and drink throughout the day. In order to respect their customs, I quickly learned that a glass of water looks just like vodka. They were toasting, and I was hydrating! I served on the joint International Space Station Commission until 2012 when I voluntarily stepped down to finally truly enjoy retirement.

Calculating formulas at NASA in 1969

My Presidential Interchange Program Profile

Dottie and the Kids in Front of Our Home in Palos Verdes, California

On the Job at Rockwell

Space Shuttle Launch – 1982

PERCY E. BAYNES
National Aeronautics & Space
  Administration
Goddard Space Flight Center
Greenbelt, Maryland 20771

Percy Baynes is the Supervisory
Mathematician Head in the Spacecraft
Control Programming Section of NASA.
His area of specialization is
computer science.

The Spacecraft Control Programming
Section is responsible for the design
and implementation of software
systems used in support of orbiting
satellites.

Baynes received a B. S. and M. S.
degree in Mathematics from Howard
University, and did additional
graduate work in the Dept. of Physics
at Maryland University.

Born in Burlington, North Carolina,
Percy Baynes is married to the
former Dorothy M. Tatten of Yancyville,
North Carolina.

NATIONAL URBAN LEAGUE, INC.

Retirement Party at NASA Headquarters - 1984

Baynes Named Director, Software Engineering

Percy E. Baynes

Percy E. Baynes joined Vitro Corporation as Director, Software Engineering on September 24, 1984. In this newly established senior position, reporting to Executive Vice President -

Baynes will be responsible for methodology that addresses a software life cycle of planning, development, and maintenance. He will direct the development of well-defined software components that document each step of the life cycle and provide traceability between steps.

Baynes comes to Vitro from the National Aeronautics and Space Administration (NASA) where he had over 20 years of software program management experience. Most recently, he was Director of the Shuttle Orbiter Division, Office of Space Flight, including management responsibility for the on-board flight software for the shuttle vehicle system.

(continued on page 2)

Article Announcing My Appointment to Vitro Corporation

Chapter Eleven
Raising Children

Start children off on the way they should go, and even when they are old they will not turn from it.
—Proverbs 22:6

For these are all our children, we will all profit by or pay for what they become.
—James Baldwin

Shortly after we were married, Dottie and I were anxious to have children and how many we wanted to have. I was locked in on having six children. When Dottie asked me, "Why six?"

I said, "Because in math, six is the smallest perfect number." I truly did see the world through mathematics! Dottie also wanted six children, because even though she was the only girl, there were six siblings in her family. We started our family in 1958.

After completing military training in Oklahoma, I went back to DC and Dottie returned to Princeton, North Carolina to fulfill her teaching contract. In late September, we discovered that she was pregnant. She completed the semester and that following February I drove to Princeton to pick her up. We loaded all her belongings and headed back north. I remember that day so well, because there was an ice storm on our way home. Our car slipped and slid all the way back to DC. Later in life, I think that's why our first baby girl, Anita, was a nervous child when she was growing up.

Anita

Anita Belinda Baynes was born on May 9, 1958, our first child and first girl. I suggested her middle name Belinda, because it was a name that I'd always liked. During the months leading up to her birth, we searched for the perfect name and decided on Anita. In Hebrew, Anita means "Grace." And even though she cried a lot (probably from that icy car ride when Dottie was pregnant), the sparkle in her eyes let us know that she was the epitome of grace.

We were so excited to be parents to baby Anita. At the time, we lived in an apartment in Southeast DC. I had just returned to work for the federal government, but my health insurance was not yet effective. So, after Anita was born, every night I'd drive my cab to earn additional money to pay our medical bill. I checked on the status of my insurance plan, and they indicated that we would be fully covered one year from Anita's birth. The timing was perfect, because Dottie was pregnant again and due the following June. We were well on our way to that perfect mathematical number—six!

Percival

Our second child, unaware of our timing for insurance coverage, decided to arrive early. Eleven months after Anita made her appearance, our first son was born on April 18, 1959. Soon after he was born, I went back to driving my taxicab at night to pay for the new medical expenses. I will never forget how my sister-cousin Mae gave us $50 toward our hospital bill. Her generosity and love meant so much to Dottie and me. We are still very close, in fact, she and Dottie do not miss a day of talking on the phone! We named our son, Percival Earl Baynes. I did not want him to be saddled with the nickname Junior, so instead, Dottie and I decided to give him my initials. (Interestingly, as an adult, Percival now prefers to go by Percy.) Dottie was only in her seventh month when he was born, so he was a small infant, but I knew that God would bless this child to grow big and strong. So, there we were, a young couple, with a boy and a girl, living in our apartment in Southeast DC.

Once Percival was old enough, five months, Dottie went back to work teaching in DC public schools. We found a great nursery school for the children and a woman that picked them up early each morning in a station wagon. In 1961, we bought our first house at 5143 12th Street, NE in Riggs Park. It was a semi detached two-story row house on a street with lots of families with small children. Families such as the Bigelow's and the Allen's would become lifelong friends. We settled in and for the next five years enjoyed raising Anita and Percival. They were so close in age; it was almost like having twins.

Steve

Still on my quest for the perfect six, Dottie and I decided to have another child. We had more space in our new home and I finally had health insurance, so I wouldn't have to drive the cab at night again to pay for the hospital bill. Our second son, Steven Todd Baynes was born on November 4, 1964. We named him Todd after someone who was very prominent at the time. My sister-cousin Mae and Dottie were pregnant at the same time—our third child and her first. The boys were born a month apart and they were so much alike; full of energy and mischief! As Steve learned to walk and then quickly run, we spent more time in the emergency room with him for various cuts and bumps.

One day, we lost Steve. We were at home and knew that he had to be close by. We started looking for him and Dottie was beginning to panic. Honestly, I was getting nervous too, but tried to remain calm, so that everyone else would. Just when we were at the height of our fear, little Steve came zooming around the block riding his tricycle down the sidewalk! His independence and sense of adventure would continue throughout his life.

Dottie took care of the kids and our household full time until Steve was two years old. She started teaching again and with three children, we were both reevaluating the idea of six being a perfect number. Perhaps six is perfect in math, but raising children was another superseding factor. However, shortly after Dottie started teaching again in the fall of 1966, we discovered that she was pregnant again!

Karen

Our fourth child, and second daughter, Karen Beatrice Baynes, was born on June 5, 1967. Anita had a doll named Karen and insisted that we name the new baby Karen as well. Dottie and I decided to honor her mother, by also giving the baby her name, Beatrice. I spent the entire night at the hospital with Dottie. As I was leaving the hospital on the morning that Karen was born I spotted a newspaper headline. A war had erupted in the Middle East between Israel and the neighboring states of Egypt, Jordan, and Syria. Bombs were exploding halfway around the world. I thought to myself, what a day for our daughter to be born. We now had four children and I bought a station wagon so that we'd have enough space to travel with our growing family.

Time to Move

We remained in our house on 12th Street until 1969. That year, I attended a session in DC regarding the state of the public school system and it was very clear to me that the system was going from bad to worse. We toyed with the idea of staying in DC and putting the kids in Catholic school. At the same time, it was also becoming evident that we needed more space. We chose to look in Montgomery County, Maryland, because the schools were highly ranked. We found a home and moved in the spring of 1969, two months before the end of school. Dottie, being the great mother that she is, drove Anita and Percival back to DC every day for a month, until the end of the school year. That summer all the kids except Karen were enrolled in Montgomery County Schools. Anita would start Junior High School at White Oak in the fall, and Percival and Steve would attend Westover Elementary School, right up the street from the house. Karen was too young for school and she would stay at home with Dottie.

The new house had a lot of space including a basement. The yard was big and there was a perfect place to plant a garden. After all those years of living in the city, I longed for the opportunity to once again grow my own vegetables. You can take the boy off the farm, but you can't take the farm out of the boy.

For the most part, the move to Maryland went well. We all had to get used to living in a predominantly white community. It had only been a year since Martin Luther King, Jr. was assassinated, and the riots erupted in DC. Once again, shortly after moving, Steve, with his sense of adventure and independence, disappeared from the backyard. We found him two doors down, in the basement of a neighbor's house, surrounded by four little white boys. At the age of five, he was singing James Brown's famous song, "Say it loud! I'm black and I'm proud!" He'd already made friends!

For Anita and Percival, the move was more difficult. They did not want to leave their friends, and Percival could not understand why we left the comfort of our all-black community and existence in DC, to move to what he referred to as the lily-white suburbs. Despite these challenges, we settled into our new life, and Dottie, who was parenting full time, helped each child adjust and begin enjoying our new neighborhood. Two years after we moved, the Allens, our neighbors from 12th Street who also had four children moved to Montgomery County, to a house that was almost next door to our home. The Allen children were like our children, and

Jennifer Allen, their oldest daughter, just happened to be Anita's best friend and another daughter in our household. All was becoming right with the world.

Traveling with the Children

The station wagon really came in handy. It was the style with the faux wood panels running down each side and it had two bumper seats in the back luggage area, allowing room to separate quarreling siblings. We made many trips to North Carolina in that wagon, to visit Daddy Waymond, Mama Bea, my sisters Vernell and Catherine, and other family members. I also liked to walk the Baynes family farm. None of my siblings wanted to continue paying taxes on the farm and had agreed to sell me their portions. I followed in my father's footsteps, who purchased his siblings' portions of the farm. On occasions, Catherine and Aunt Myrtle would accompany us back to Maryland. The kids all loved it when they came to visit. Steve especially liked my sister's famous chocolate pies and used to laugh uncontrollably whenever he said, "Ant Cat!" All the kids used to gather around and listen to Aunt Myrtle recite poetry she remembered from her childhood.

In 1970, we decided to drive the children to vacation in Miami, Florida. We chose Miami, because unlike most of the other segregated cities in Florida, Miami was a city that seemed to be open to all races of people.

At the time, I loved taking family movies on an eight-millimeter film camera that Dottie bought me for Christmas. I was filming the family toward the end of a visit to the Miami Zoo, when our youngest, Karen, decided she was not ready to leave. She plopped herself down on the ground and refused to move. We left her sitting on the ground and after a while, she started to slowly scoot herself along the ground toward us. It was one of the many hilarious and special moments that I caught on film. We also went to the beach while in Miami and had a lot of fun.

On the way home, I was intent on not stopping and having my family experience the unrelenting racism and malicious Jim Crow laws that still loomed in the Deep South. Dottie was upset with me, but I could not deal with the blatant discrimination that seemed to intensify after King was assassinated. Most of all, I did not want our children exposed to it. I wanted them to enjoy the innocence of childhood for as long as possible. We drove 845 miles straight through to Yanceyville. We must have stopped for gas along the way, but I don't remember how I determined which gas stations were safe.

Child Rearing

As I was busy with my career at NASA, Dottie was the primary parent taking the kids to all their activities and appointments. When Karen turned four, Dottie began teaching again. I knew that she was the love of my life, but she was also an extraordinary mother. She instinctively knew that the children should experience things like museums, plays, and trips to the library. She made sure that they were each exposed to music and the arts, Anita took dance and piano, Percival learned violin and excelled in art, Steve learned violin and piano, and Karen learned piano and the clarinet.

When time permitted, I became involved with some of the children's activities as well. For two years, I served as the assistant troop leader for the Boy Scouts with Percival and Steve. One year, we went on a winter camping trip in Shenandoah. I am not sure who thought this would be a good idea. We camped in the snow, and it was the coldest I think I have ever been (and that's saying a lot for someone who grew up in a log home with no central heat). I also served as the manager/coach for Percival's recreation league football team in 1973 and Steve's baseball team in 1980. Both the boys were extremely gifted athletes and very responsive to my direction. I cherished those moments, watching them both excel. As all the children continued to grow and blossom, we were blessed to see each of them graduate from Springbrook High School.

After graduating high school in 1976, the nation's centennial celebration year, Anita went to Towson State College in Baltimore before transferring to Maryland University at College Park to complete her degree in education (following in the footsteps of her mother). She was still dating her high school sweetheart, Todd Ellis, who enlisted in the U.S. Marine Corps. During her junior year in college, Todd came to our house and asked me for Anita's hand in marriage. He explained that they would wait until she graduated from college to get married. I remember thinking, and I may have even said it out loud, "Why wait? Get married now, and you can pay for her last year in college!" Over the years, Todd has become a part of our family and through the Marine Corps they have traveled the world. Anita also earned her master's degree in education and has served as an extraordinary middle school teacher for nearly 40 years. She and Todd have one daughter, who graduated from Hampton University, and two precocious grandsons.

After graduating high school in 1977, Percival chose to attend Frostburg College in Salisbury, Maryland. I remember thinking about how cold it was in the mountains of Maryland and wondered if it was a good fit for him. At the end of his freshman year, unbeknownst to us, Percival enlisted in the U.S. Air Force. In fact, we didn't know he did it until the day before he was going to his induction ceremony. He served for four years, which included an assignment in Italy. His desire was to become a pilot, which was also my dream as a college student. Unfortunately, he had hearing loss in one ear, which meant he could not pursue the pilot track. He came out of the Air Force in 1981, with the GI Bill and enrolled at Shaw University (also following in the footsteps of his mother). He later transferred to NC Central and completed his degree in history. He continues to live in North Carolina and has three daughters, three granddaughters, and two grandsons.

Upon graduating high school in 1982, Steve was accepted into the Coast Guard Academy, ranked among the nation's most elite undergraduate colleges. He was one of a handful of black students in his class and he thrived both in the classroom (majoring in math, following in the footsteps of his father) and on the football field. He was commissioned as an officer and served our country for 27 years. His assignments took him to the jungles of Bolivia in a joint effort with the Drug Enforcement Agency, to the shores of California, Florida, and the Gulf Coast. He was the Captain of the first cutter deployed when Hurricane Katrina bored down on New Orleans and Mississippi. The Coast Guard paid for Steve to obtain his master's degree in analytics and he also spent a year as a scholar in residence with the Brookings Institute. Steve retired from the Coast Guard as a Captain in 2010. He has two sons.

During her senior year in high school, in 1985, there were many colleges recruiting Karen. I thought she would go to the University of Maryland at College Park that offered her a full scholarship package out of this world. In fact, I tried to bribe her indicating that she could then use the college money we saved to buy the Mazda RX7 she loved. For some reason, she didn't want to go to a large school, and instead chose to attend Wake Forest University in Winston-Salem, North Carolina. In retrospect, it turned out to be a good choice for her, as she was honored to study with the famous author and poet Maya Angelou and spent a semester in Liberia, West Africa. I thought that she would major in physics, because she was good at it. She called one day and announced that she was switching her major to political science. I didn't know she wanted to go to law school. I told her and all the children that I would pay for only four years of college. But when she shared her vision of going to law school, I changed my mind and paid for it also. She chose Berkeley—another strange choice in my mind—but she was successful, and she graduated. We were overjoyed. I sent Karen and Dottie to Hawaii as a graduation gift. During their trip, I called them at the hotel and left a message, "Please tell Karen Baynes, Esquire, that she has passed the bar!" Karen went on to practice law and serve as a judge. She has two sons.

All our children are doing well, and they are raising their children to know God and to appreciate family. We pray that they continue their good work and remember that it is what Christ has already done for them.

Dottie at Aunt Delsie's house and Anita, Percival and me in 1960

The Kids in Yanceyville, North Carolina in 1969

Our Last Christmas Living on 12th Street

Dottie and the Kids during Our Trip to Miami in the Station Wagon

Chapter Twelve
Rebuilding the Totten Homestead

For every house is built by someone, but God is the builder of everything.
—Hebrews 3:4

If you want to lift yourself up, lift up someone else.
—Booker T. Washington

In March 1975, the Totten family home burned to the ground. The fire was caused by sparks escaping from holes in the chimney. Daddy Waymond had decorated the upstairs by placing brown paper on all the walls. A spark from the chimney ignited the paper and destroyed the entire home.

The Totten home was a two-story, white-framed structure, filled with antique furniture, with a front porch and a screened in area off the back. It sat on a 406-acre tobacco farm in Yanceyville, North Carolina. They moved from Rabbit Shuffle to their new home in 1970. To say that it was unusual for a black family to own this much land and this type of house in North Carolina at that time is a gross understatement. Their acquisition of this sprawling farm and all its assets was the talk of the county and probably the state for years to come.

The Harrelson sisters, two white women, were the previous owners. Neither sister ever married nor had children. Daddy Waymond and Mama Bea worked for the sisters. He tended the farm and the land, while she took care of the house. Their friends and family thought the Totten's were crazy for working for these two eccentric women. The sisters paid very little, expected very much, and annually rewarded them with used cookware and other such items for Christmas.

Eventually, Molly Harrelson died, and her sister Annie Harrelson took ill. Despite having six children to still care for in Rabbit Shuffle, Mama Bea moved into the house with Annie to care for her, while Daddy Waymond continued running the farm. On her deathbed, Annie Harrelson called Daddy Waymond to her bedside and told him that she was leaving the entire farm and everything on it to him. She even told him where she hid money in the house, so that he could pay the estate taxes, and no one could take it away from him.

The white townspeople were outraged. North Carolina was part of the Jim Crow South. In fact, the courthouse in the Yanceyville square was infamous for the Ku Klux Klan murder of John Stephens in 1870. (*Stephens was a Republican State Senator and Justice of the Peace from Caswell County, who was trying to get blacks to vote for Republican candidates.*) The same store owners and salesmen who previously provided Daddy Waymond with farm supplies while he was taking care of the land for the Harrelson sisters, now refused to sell to him. And yet, through sheer determination, faith, and hard work, Daddy Waymond and Mama Bea survived and prospered. While never viewed as a wealthy family, they provided for all their children and produced tobacco on the land that helped employ and feed their extended family and friends as well.

So, in March 1975, when the Totten home burned to the ground, it was devastating for everyone. Fortunately, it happened during the day so no one was home except Mama Bea and Dottie's first cousin Christine and her son Sean. It was Christine who called us. She simply said, "The house has burned down."

Dottie and I drove to Yanceyville, not knowing what we would find. The only things they were able to save were a sofa, a chair, and one or two other items. The antique furniture brought from Rabbit Shuffle and most of the items given to the Totten family by the Harrelson sisters had gone up in flames. The fire was so intense that even bags of silver coins melted and stuck together. Daddy Waymond, who was such a hardworking and proud family man seemed broken. When we arrived, I'll never forget seeing and feeling the sadness and pain on their faces. At that moment, I felt like someone punched me in the stomach. It was a moment that would have rocked the faith of the strongest Christian. I was overwhelmed with the desire to help them rebuild. The local men, including Daddy Waymond's brothers, were talking about cutting logs to rebuild the house, which would have taken a year and half. I wanted to get them back into the house as quickly as possible.

The issue confronting them was whether they would move back to the house in Rabbit Shuffle on 62 or try to rebuild. There was not enough insurance to rebuild, so the choice seemed inevitable. Prior to the fire, Dottie and I had planned to build a summer house on Badgett Sisters Parkway, around the corner from the site of the fire. We'd already surveyed and obtained building permits. We even perked for a well. None of that mattered.

At the time, I was a GS-15 with the federal government. God blessed me to have all my financial commitments under control, and we saved money. It was so clear that God was once again working in mysterious ways. It was spiritual—to whom much is given, much is expected. Rather than building our house, we decided to rebuild the Totten family home and give Daddy Waymond and Mama Bea lifetime occupancy. We entered into a contract with a builder to build the house.

I interfaced with the builder to select several plans and Daddy Waymond and Mama Bea chose the one they liked the most. Mamma Bea thought it would be bad luck to rebuild the house on the exact same location, so we worked with the builder to build the house to the left of the original plot and turned the house around so that the front door faced west instead of south. All the debris from the old house was removed and buried.

While the house was being built, Dottie's parents lived down the street with her brother Ervin and his wife Florine. Jackie, Dottie's niece (who is more like her little sister) was supposed to get married that summer, so the wedding was moved to Ervin and Florine's house as well. After eight months, the house was finished, we bought furniture and they moved back in.

God saw fit that we never experienced any problems continuing to pay tithes to the church while paying for their house and meeting our family's obligations in Silver Spring, Maryland. In fact, God enabled us to double up our payments and we paid off the 20-year mortgage in ten years.

In 1979, Daddy Waymond asked to speak to me. With the lifetime occupancy we granted them, he was still feeling as though he was living under another man's roof. I understood. I imagine my father would have felt the same way. We transferred the house over to them in exchange for 100 acres of additional land on Badgett Sisters Parkway. The land was rather inexpensive. The mortgage on the house was $50K. In 1979, they were living in their house with a title and Daddy Waymond was filled with joy. Before they died, the house was completely paid off.

In 1996, Mama Bea and Daddy Waymond decided to write their wills. They divided the farm up among their living children and made provisions for Scooter and Jack's children, two of Dottie's brothers who died years earlier. There were three acres on which the new house was built, and they decided that those three acres and the house would also be left to Dottie. I didn't want any more land, but no one else wanted to pay the taxes. So, we ended up with seventy additional acres for a total of one hundred seventy-eight acres of land.

After Daddy Waymond and Mama Bea died, Dottie and I started spending more time in Yanceyville during the summers. We eventually decided to move back to Yanceyville, the home I had left sixty-one years before on a Greyhound bus headed to DC.

Beatrice Totten (Mama Bea) and her siblings, Matokia, Lula Mae and Georgia in the Totten

homestead before the fire

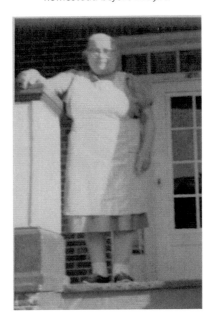

Miss Annie Harrelson

Mama Bea and Daddy Waymond in the newspaper for growing the largest watermelon in the county

The Caswell Messenger, Inc., Thursday, September 9, 1982

65 Pounds! It was a good year for watermelons for Waymond and Beatrice Totten Yanceyville, who grew this 65 pound watermelon in their garden this year.

Chapter Thirteen
Returning Home to North Carolina: "Your father has lived his life, and that he has done. You have yours yet to live."

Then the LORD said to Jacob, "Return to the land of your fathers and to your relatives, and I will be with you."
—Genesis 31:3

But why had he always felt so strongly the magnetic pull of home, why had he thought so much about it and remembered it with such blazing accuracy, if it did not matter, and if this little town, and the immortal hills around it, was not the only home he had on earth? He did not know. All that he knew was that the years flow by like water, and that one day men come home again.
—Thomas Wolfe, *You Can't Go Home Again*

When I left North Carolina on September 15, 1950, I had $600 stuffed in my front pocket on my way to Washington, DC. When I returned in 2011, God blessed us beyond measure. This book chronicles my journey up and back. I was part of the Great Migration, when 6 million African Americans moved from the rural South to urban cities in the Northeast, Midwest, and West between 1916 and 1971. Washington, DC was heavily populated by North and South Carolinians for many reasons. First, many already had family members there. A second factor was that segregation laws in DC were not as hardened as the South. Finally, and perhaps the number one reason was jobs—not factory jobs like most cities, but federal government jobs. It was that professional journey through NASA, the spiritual growth at First Baptist Church, and the extraordinary friends that we made along the way that led us to stay. Despite the life we built in DC and Silver Spring, Maryland, after 61 years, it was time to go home.

By 2011, I retired from my good federal government job as well as the private sector and I wanted a more relaxed living arrangement. Sitting in traffic on four hundred ninety-five diminished my quality of life and I desired to live in a rural area that would be comfortable and free of smog and car exhaust. On those long commutes, I often thought about home and could almost smell the tobacco smoking in the barn.

I planned well for retirement, so we were blessed with the resources to think about making a move. We weren't sure if we could go from living in DC back to the rural life of Yanceyville, so Dottie and I started looking for homes in Greensboro, North Carolina, about 45 miles west of Yanceyville. Greensboro was the site of the famous lunch counter sit-ins during the 1960s Civil Rights Movement.

I remember going looking at homes and not seeing anything that we liked. Even in the late 1990s, Greensboro was still very segregated. So, we decided to build a summer home in Yanceyville. I still thought of the Totten family home as Daddy Waymond and Mama Bea's—a place where family came together. So, I didn't contemplate moving into their home, even though they were both deceased by 2000. In the end, however, the only thing that made sense was to move into the Totten family home.

At first, my plan was to expand the house by making the kitchen into a recreation room and moving the kitchen to the carport area. Dottie brought me back to my senses and made me realize that unlike our previous hectic household filled with four children and all their friends, it would now just be the two of us. We decided to open the wall between the living room and dining room and built a room under the sunroom. A comfortable home on land filled with memories, the beauty of family, and the grace of God.

I have to admit that we did have some concerns about moving back to the country such as: finding a church home; adjusting to rural life without the commercial amenities nearby and without our friends; and navigating ice and thunderstorms, which often knocked out electricity in the Yanceyville region. We joined my old home church, where I continued to serve as a Deacon. It is also the place where my parents, grandparents, and many of my relatives are buried. I am constantly inspired by their presence and spirits. We love the slower pace of life, we stay in touch with our friends in the DC area, and unlike when we lived in North Carolina as children, we now realize that Danville, Virginia and Burlington, North Carolina are only a hop, skip, and a jump away. Finally, we installed a generator that automatically turns on when we lose electricity. The electrician, Mack Bingham, refused to accept any payment beyond the parts needed to install it (another beautiful and gracious note about people living in a small country town). It has worked without fail! Through the years, the Totten homestead has continued to be a gathering place for our family and friends.

For many years, we had a paperback version of Thomas Wolfe's book, *You Can't Go Home Again*. Wolfe was also born in North Carolina. His novel told the story of an author who tried to return to his hometown only to discover that it was not the same as he remembered it. There was much about growing up in Caswell County that was difficult—especially the memories of my parents' deaths and the discrimination toward black people. However, I never lost my affinity for the land. The rich life lessons conveyed during tobacco harvest, Sunday mornings at Sweet Gum Baptist Church, and driving the school bus laid the foundation that carried me through the sixty-one years that Dottie and I worked and raised our family in DC and Maryland.

I knew that it would not be the same. The world had changed tremendously over the decades since our Great Migration north. Becoming part of the reverse Black Great Migration back to the South seemed to be exactly what we needed at this point in our lives. Our children were all successful adults and enjoying their own families. God blessed us with resources that would more than support our retirement. Finally, there was something about clean air, no traffic, and a simpler way of life that attracted us. We changed and our hometown changed. We were not returning to be tobacco farmers—we were returning to a landmark, once used as a tobacco farm —but with a new perspective about its use. The one hundred seventy-six acres and home house on the Totten farm and the ninety acres originally purchased by my grandfather, then from my father (from his siblings), and then purchased by me (from my siblings), were ripe with possibilities to develop a place where our families and other people of all races, ethnicities, and religions could come relax, reflect, and revive. Our return would not be a contradiction to Thomas Wolfe, but a reimagining of our hometown with an express purpose.

We raised our children to think about others and always be civically engaged, and they are the ones that came up with the idea of using the farm to create opportunities for children to be children—especially those involved in public systems and those whose parents were experiencing homelessness. Our children reminisced about their summers on the farm and desired to introduce the beauty of rural living to the next generation. They wanted to bring people and families together to pass on the experience that I had growing up on that land. What an investment by my grandfather in 1914—to buy a landlocked farm. The kids, Dottie, and I decided to build a retreat log home and develop a plan to build out the farm with other facilities over time.

I converted the farm to a Limited Liability Corporation named the Baynes Family Farm, LLC. The first construction was a pavilion in 2012, and then we dug out a new pond that same year. A local contractor, Wesley McKinney, did the construction and built heavy duty picnic tables that should last another hundred years. Fred E. Williamson, who lives down the street, assisted by providing lawn fertilization and plowed the garden. My new friend, Glen Wilson, did the landscaping and sewed the grass seeds to create a blanket of lush green. When I left North Carolina, all being of different races, we would never have been friends. Upon my return, I count Glen as one of my closest friends in Caswell County. I returned to my hometown with a different mind-set, different relationships, and an enriched experience.

When I was a boy, poor white people would come and help black people shuck corn. After a long day of work, in our very own kitchens, the white workers would eat first. Only after they had finished eating could we enter our own kitchens to eat. Back then, you could stand beside white people to work, but not to eat. Times had certainly changed when I returned. My friendship with Glen inspired me to develop a retreat center that would be open to all races and all ethnicities to reflect this new enriched reality.

Years earlier, the Children's Defense Fund purchased Alex Haley's family farm outside of Knoxville, Tennessee. They restored the home house and built or renovated other buildings on the land to accommodate large groups of people working toward social justice and equity. I saw pictures of it and thought we could develop something similar on the Baynes Family Farm.

That same summer, we held a Baynes Family Reunion themed: *From the Roots to the Branches: Uplifting the Baynes Legacy*. Under the newly built pavilion we revealed our vision for the farm to extended family members and friends.

Dottie, the kids, and I looked through what seemed like hundreds of log home plans and finally settled on one that we all loved and slightly modified it to add an additional full bathroom. It is strange to think that three full bathrooms would not be enough, given that the last time I lived on the land we didn't have any indoor bathrooms!

In 2013, we began construction on the main log home. I didn't want it to be directly on the site of my grandfather's house. So, we built it in a field about a hundred yards west of that original site, overlooking the pond. The home faces north and has a wraparound porch. There are unobstructed views of breathtaking sunrises and extraordinary sunsets. There is always a refreshing crosswind no matter where you stand. I believe that constant breeze contains the spirits of my ancestors who continue to watch over us.

Once the contractor excavated and dug out the basement in preparation for the building, all six of us got together to bless the land. We offered libations to our ancestors and to God. In that moment, I was so grateful: Grateful to God for allowing us to be together on this land for which I have always held such an affinity; and grateful that over the years, when there was nothing to see but my grandfather's house which was collapsing and infested with weeds, snakes, and who knows what—and what was left of my little birth house, I used to walk the land with my children. I told them stories of growing up on the farm and in the segregated Jim Crow South. Despite the loss of family members over the years, I have rich memories, family, and love. I met and married the love of my life, not far from where we stood. Here we gathered with our four adult children, over fifty years after we had married and over sixty years after we first met. I never knew Thomas Wolfe personally, but I wish that he could have been with us on this day. The libation ceremony was adapted from the Kwanza Libation Statement written by Maulana Karenga:

Our fathers and mothers came here, lived, loved, struggled and built here. At this place, their love and labor rose like the sun and gave strength and meaning to the day.

For them, then, who gave so much we give in return. On this same soil we will sow our seeds, and liberation and a higher level of human life. May our eyes be the eagle, our strength be the elephant, and the boldness of our life be like the lion. And may we remember and honor our ancestors and the legacy they left for as long as the sun shines and the waters flow.
For our people everywhere then:

For our African ancestors and all the others known and unknown who defended our ancestral land, history, and humanity from alien invaders;

For Garvey, Muhammad, Malcolm, and King; Harriet, Fannie Lou, Sojourner, Bethune, and Nat Turner and all the others who dared to define, defend, and develop our interests as a people;

For George and Rebecca, Charlie and Mary, who worked this land, stood on faith in raising their families, and planted seeds of shade trees under which they would never stand;

For Catherine, John, Dad, and Vernell who made it possible for us to be here today to continue on our family's valiant struggle for the liberation and vindication of our people;

For our children and their children and the fuller and freer lives they will live because we struggle;

For the new world we struggle to build and the lives that will forever be impacted by this home and this vision;

And for the continuing struggle through which we will inevitably rescue and reconstruct our history and humanity in God's own image and purpose.
For these and all other blessings, we thank God today and every day.

In May 2014, one hundred years after my grandfather first purchased the farm, we dedicated the log home. We opened it for guests in August that same year. My son Steve decided to post the log home on Airbnb and VRBO, thinking it might be attractive for those wanting a special place to relax or celebrate. Immediately people of all races, ethnicities, and persuasions started booking time at the farm for family reunions, birthday celebrations, weddings, and even corporate team building. In fact, there is rarely a weekend when the home is not booked.

In 2015, we built a caretaker's house, where our son Percival now resides. The proceeds from rentals were such a blessing, that the kids moved forward with their original vision of using the farm to nurture children. During the summer of 2017, we hosted the first Camp Phoenix for children of homeless families. Working with a nonprofit partner in Durham, North Carolina, we hosted fifteen of the most precious and precocious seven to eleven year olds. The camp continues and gets bigger and better each year.

I am so proud to see our children working together to make the world a better place. I am so proud that the legacy started by my ancestors continues in each of them and now in their children.

The farm has blessed our family for over a century and it is now also a blessing for surrounding businesses who our guests patronize while relaxing, reflecting, and reviving in Caswell County, North Carolina.

The circle is now complete. I was born in Caswell County and I have returned to Caswell County. At the age of eighty-six, there is something about returning to the place of one's birth that is so incredibly profound. On June 6, 1949, the day my father died, I laid in the gully behind my grandfather's house and had an epiphany. The Lord spoke to me so clearly that day. "Your father has lived his life, and that he has done. You have yours yet to live." Over the sixty-one years of my sojourn to the DC area God blessed me to live a life of purpose. I returned to my home, my very own launch site, with a new perspective, a new understanding of the world, and a deeper appreciation for my family and the way in which I was raised.

They say that everything happens for a reason. The pain of losing my parents at such a young age propelled me forward and enabled me to take the risk of stepping out on faith. Along the way, God used people in my life such as Dottie, Uncle Ernest, Aunt Delsie, Cousin Mae, my First Baptist family, coworkers, friends, and children to keep me grounded and continue giving me the greatest gift of all—Love.

To God be the Glory!

Bob Jones, Thomas Vanhook and me at the Baynes General Store in 1994

Walking the Baynes Family Farm

My Friend Wesley McKinney

The Baynes Family Farm in 2019

Postscript

For my wife Dottie,

You have always known that I have a favorite song. However, you probably don't know why it means so much to me. Every time I hear this song, it makes me think about you and our life together. I know that this journey has not always been easy, but I also know that without you by my side, none of this would have been possible. Together, over the past 62 years, we have raised four wonderful children, and we now have a host of grandchildren and great-grandchildren. We have both been successful in our careers, and we have helped a lot of other people along the way. I may have received a lot of accolades, especially during my time at NASA, but you are the true hero in this story. Your loving sacrifices and quiet resolve have kept me focused, created beauty in our household, and there was not a day that I did not feel your love, devotion, and support. Dottie, my favorite song is about you . . . you are the wind beneath my wings.

Love,

Percy

Wind Beneath My Wings

Songwriters: Jeff Silbar / Larry Henley / Larry J. Henley

It must have been cold there in my shadow,
To never have sunlight on your face.
You were content to let me shine, that's your way.
You always walked a step behind.

So I was the one with all the glory,
While you were the one with all the strength.
A beautiful face without a name for so long.
A beautiful smile to hide the pain.

Did you ever know that you're my hero,
And everything I would like to be?
I can fly higher than an eagle,
For you are the wind beneath my wings.

It might have appeared to go unnoticed,
But I've got it all here in my heart.
I want you to know I know the truth, of course I know it.
I would be nothing without you.

Did you ever know that you're my hero?
You're everything I wish I could be.
I could fly higher than an eagle,
For you are the wind beneath my wings.

Did I ever tell you you're my hero?
You're everything, everything I wish I could be.
Oh, and I, I could fly higher than an eagle,
For you are the wind beneath my wings,
'cause you are the wind beneath my wings.

Oh, the wind beneath my wings.
You, you, you, you are the wind beneath my wings.
Fly, fly, fly away. You let me fly so high.
Oh, you, you, you, the wind beneath my wings.
Oh, you, you, you, the wind beneath my wings.

Fly, fly, fly high against the sky,
So high I almost touch the sky.
Thank you, thank you,
Thank God for you, the wind beneath my wings.

photograph taken by Kimberly Gibson

Made in the USA
Middletown, DE
24 October 2020